ROWAN

Panama Collection

15 designs for women using Panama
by Marie Wallin, Lisa Richardson & Grace Melville

Guava
By Marie Wallin
Pattern Page 48

Passion
By Marie Wallin
Pattern Page 57

Mangosteen
By Grace Melville
Pattern Page 54

Prickly Pear
By Marie Wallin
Pattern Page 64

Banana Wrap
By Lisa Richardson
Pattern Page 37

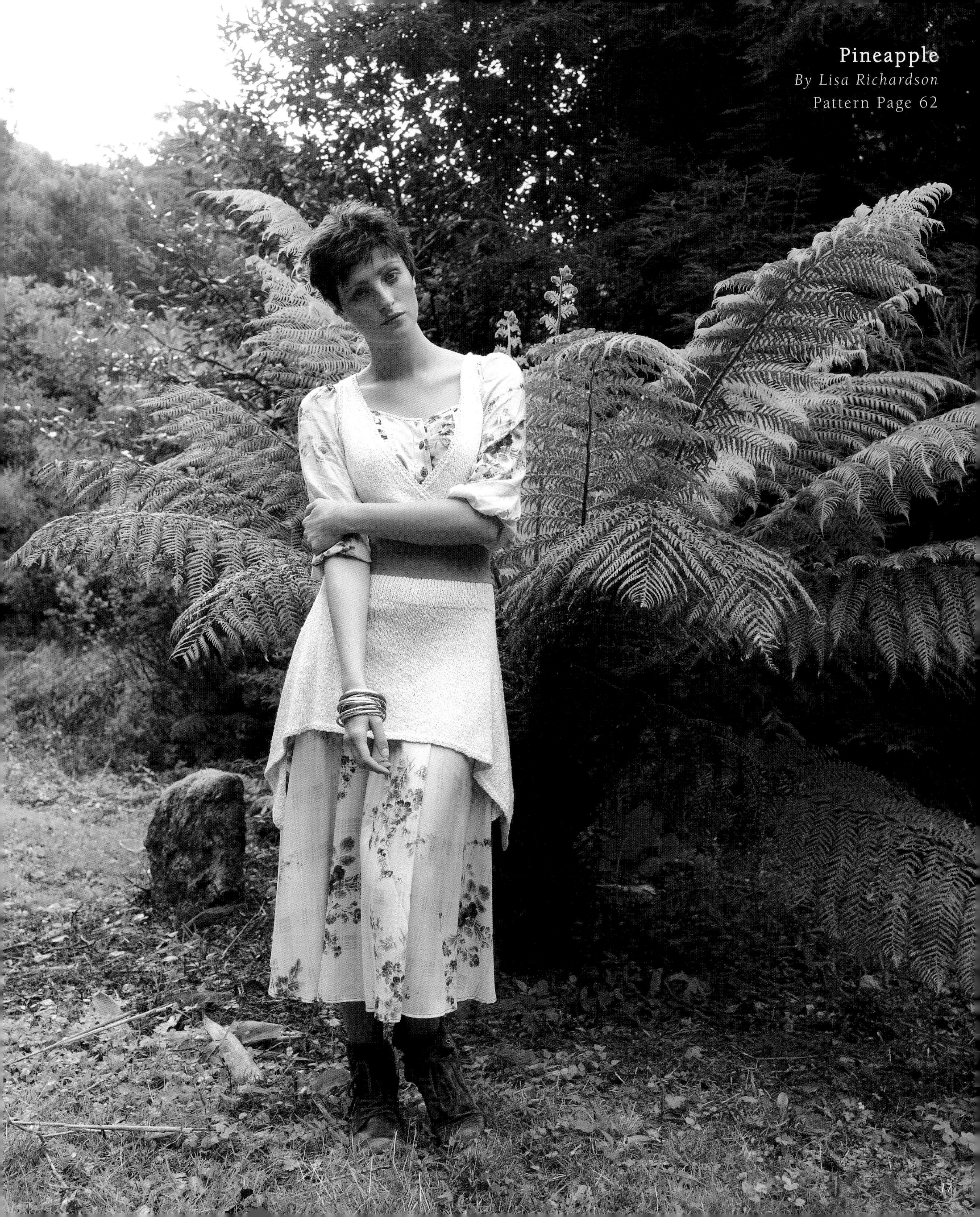

Pineapple

By Lisa Richardson

Pattern Page 62

Candlenut
By Grace Melville
Pattern Page 41

Mango
By Lisa Richardson
Pattern Page 52

Apricot
By Marie Wallin
Pattern Page 34

25

Kaffir Dress
By Lisa Richardson
Pattern Page 49

Carob
By Marie Wallin
Pattern Page 42

Papaya
By Grace Melville
Pattern Page 55

Bread Fruit
By Lisa Richardson
Pattern Page 38

Apricot ✹✹✹
By Marie Wallin

Main Image Page 22

SIZE

S	M	L	XL	XXL	
To fit bust					
81–86	91–97	102–107	112–117	122–127	cm
32–34	36–38	40–42	44–46	48–50	in

YARN

Rowan Panama

14	15	17	19	21	x 50gm

(photographed in Daisy 301)

CROCHET HOOK

2.50mm (no 11) (US C2) crochet hook

BUTTONS - 6 x RW5022 (15mm) from Bedecked. See information page for contact details.

TENSION

3 patt reps (30 sts) and 4 patt reps (16 rows) to **12** cm measured over patt using 2.50mm (US C2) crochet hook.

CROCHET ABBREVIATIONS

ss = slip stitch; **ch** = chain; **dc** = double crochet; **tr** = treble; **dtr** = double treble; **ttr** = triple treble; **sp(s)** = space(s); **back double** = 4 ch, without turning work (thereby working backwards) miss last 6 dc just worked, 1 ss into 7th dc, now working in original direction work 5 dc into ch sp just formed; **tr3tog** = ★yoh and insert hook as indicated, yoh and draw loop through, yoh and draw through 2 loops, rep from ★ twice more, yoh and draw through all 4 loops on hook; **yoh** = yarn over hook.

BACK

Using 2.50mm (US C2) hook make 129 [139: 159: 169: 189] ch.
Foundation row (WS): 1 dc into 14th ch from hook, ★5 ch, miss 4 ch, 1 tr into next ch★★, 5 ch, miss 4 ch, 1 dc into next ch, rep from ★ to end, ending last rep at ★★, turn. 12 [13: 15: 16: 18] patt reps.
Now work in patt as folls:
Row 1 (RS): 1 ch (does NOT count as st), 1 dc into first tr, ★6 dc into next ch sp, 1 dc into next dc, (3 dc, 1 back double and 3 dc) into next ch sp, 1 dc into next tr, rep from ★ to end, working dc at end of last rep into 3rd of 8 ch at beg of previous row, turn. (**Note:** On this first rep of patt row 1, this "3rd of 8 ch" will be the 6th ch beyond the first dc of the foundation row.)
Row 2: 1 ch (does NOT count as st), 1 dc into first dc, ★5 ch, 1 tr into centre dc of 5 dc of back double, 5 ch, 1 dc into dc directly above tr of last-but-one row, rep from ★ to end, working last dc into last dc, turn.
Row 3: 1 ch (does NOT count as st), 1 dc into first dc, 3 dc into first 5-ch sp, turn, 2 ch, miss 3 dc just worked, 1 tr into first dc, turn, 1 ch (does NOT count as st), 1 dc into tr, 2 dc into 2-ch sp just formed. 3 dc into same 5-ch sp as 3 dc at beg of row, ★1 dc into next tr, 6 dc into next ch sp, 1 dc into next dc★★, (3 dc, 1 back double and 3 dc) into next ch sp, rep from ★ to end, ending last rep at ★★, 5 ch, miss last 3 dc, 1 ss into 4th dc, 3 dc into ch sp just formed, turn.
Row 4: 8 ch (counts as 1 tr and 5 ch), ★1 dc into dc directly above tr of last-but-one row, 5 ch★★, 1 tr into centre dc of 5 dc of back double, 5 ch, rep from ★ to end, ending last rep at ★★, 1 tr into last dc, turn.
These 4 rows form patt.
Work 2 rows, ending after patt row 2 and with RS facing for next row.
Dec row 1 (RS): 1 ch (does NOT count as st), 1 dc into first dc, 6 dc into first ch sp, 1 dc into next tr, patt until 1 dc has been worked into first tr of previous row, 6 dc into next ch sp, 1 dc into last dc, turn.
Dec row 2: Ss along and into dc directly above tr of last-but-one row, 1 ch (does NOT count as st), 1 dc into same dc as last ss – ½ patt rep decreased, 5 ch, 1 tr into centre dc of 5 dc of back double, patt until dc has been worked into dc directly above last tr of last-but-one row, turn, leaving rem sts unworked – ½ patt rep decreased. 11 [12: 14: 15: 17] patt reps.
Beg with patt row 3, work 4 [4: 4: 8: 8] rows, ending after patt row 2 and with RS facing for next row.
Rep dec rows 1 and 2 once more. 10 [11: 13: 14: 16] patt reps.
Beg with patt row 3, work 12 [16: 16: 16: 20] rows, ending after patt row 2 and with RS facing for next row.
Inc row 1 (RS): Remove hook from working loop. Using separate ball of yarn attach yarn to **beg** of previous row, 6 ch and fasten off. Pick up working loop at end of previous row again and work across row as folls: 7 ch, 2 dc into 2nd ch from hook, 1 dc into next of next 5 ch, 1 dc into next dc, (3 dc, 1 back double and 3 dc) into next ch sp – ½ patt rep

increased, patt until dc has been worked into last dc, now work across length of ch attached to beg of previous row as folls: 1 dc into each of next 3 ch, 1 back double, 1 dc into each of next 2 ch, 2 dc into last ch - ½ patt rep increased, turn. 11 [12: 14: 15: 17] patt reps.

Beg with patt row 2, work 17 rows, ending after patt row 2 and with RS facing for next row.

Shape armholes

Working all decreases as set by side seam decreases, shape armholes as folls:

Rep dec rows 1 and 2, 3 [3: 5: 5: 6] times. 8 [9: 9: 10: 11] patt reps.

Beg with patt row 3, work 20 rows, ending after patt row 2 and with RS facing for next row.

Shape back neck

Next row (RS): Work 2 [2½: 2: 2½: 3] patt reps and turn, leaving rem sts unworked.

Work 1 row on these 2 [2½: 2: 2½: 3] patt reps.

Fasten off.

Return to last complete row worked, miss centre 4 [4: 5: 5: 5] patt reps, attach yarn to st at beg of next patt rep and patt to end. 2 [2½: 2: 2½: 3] patt reps.

Work 1 row.

Fasten off.

LEFT FRONT

Using 2.50mm (US C2) hook make 69 [79: 89: 89: 99] ch.

Work foundation row as given for back. 6 [7: 8: 8: 9] patt reps.

Now work in patt as given for back for 6 rows, ending after patt row 2 and with RS facing for next row.

Working all shaping as given for back, dec ½ patt rep at side seam edge (beg of next row) over next 2 rows. 5½ [6½: 7½: 7½: 8½] patt reps.

Work 4 [4: 4: 8: 8] rows, ending with RS facing for next row.

Dec ½ patt rep at side seam edge (beg of next row) over next 2 rows. 5 [6: 7: 7: 8] patt reps.

Work 12 [16: 16: 16: 20] rows, ending with RS facing for next row.

Inc ½ patt rep at beg of next row. 5½ [6½: 7½: 7½: 8½] patt reps.

Work 17 rows, ending with RS facing for next row.

Shape armhole

Dec ½ patt rep at armhole edge over next 2 rows.

Rep last 2 rows 2 [2: 4: 4: 5] times. 4 [5: 5: 5: 5½] patt reps.

Work 9 rows, ending with **WS** facing for next row.

Shape front neck

Fasten off.

With **WS** facing, miss first ½ [1½: 1½: 1½: 1] patt reps, attach yarn to dc at beg of next patt rep, 1 ch (does NOT count as st), 1 dc into same place as where yarn was rejoined, patt to end, turn. 3½ [3½: 3½: 3½: 4½] patt reps.

Next row (RS): Work 3 [3: 3: 3: 4] full pat reps and turn, leaving rem ½ patt rep unworked.

Work 1 row, ending after patt row 2.

Dec ½ patt rep at neck edge over next 2 rows. 2 [2½: 2: 2½: 3] patt reps.

Work 6 [8: 6: 8: 6] rows, ending with RS facing for next row.

Fasten off.

RIGHT FRONT

Work to match left front, reversing shapings.

SLEEVES

Using 2.50mm (US C2) hook make 69 [69: 79: 79: 79] ch.

Work foundation row as given for back. 6 [6: 7: 7: 7] patt reps.

Now work in patt as given for back for 6 [6: 10: 10: 10] rows, ending after patt row 2 and with RS facing for next row.

Working all shaping as given for back, inc ½ patt rep at each end of next row. 7 [7: 8: 8: 8] patt reps.

Beg with patt row 2, work 9 rows, ending after patt row 2 and with RS facing for next row.

Rep last 10 rows twice more, then first of these 10 rows (the inc row) again. 10 [10: 11: 11: 11] patt reps.

Beg with patt row 2, work 9 rows, ending after patt row 2 and with RS facing for next row.

Shape top

Dec ½ patt rep at each end over next 2 rows.

Rep last 2 rows 6 [6: 7: 7: 7] times more. 4 patt reps.

Fasten off.

MAKING UP

Press as described on the information page.

Join both shoulder seams using back stitch.

Collar

Using 2.50mm (US C2) hook make 169 [168: 179: 179: 179] ch.

Work foundation row as given for back. 16 [16: 17: 17: 17] patt reps.

Now work in patt as given for back for 10 rows, ending after patt row 2 and with RS facing for next row.

Place markers at both ends of last row.

Working all shaping as given for back, dec ½ patt rep at each end over next 2 rows.

Rep last 2 rows once more. 14 [14: 15: 15: 15] patt reps.

Fasten off.

Button band

With RS facing and using 2.50mm (US C2) hook, attach yarn at top of left front opening edge and work as folls:

Row 1 (RS): 1 ch (does NOT count as st), work a row of dc evenly down entire left front opening edge, ensuring number of dc worked is a multiple of 10 plus one extra, turn.

Row 2: 1 ch (does NOT count as st), 1 dc into each dc to end, turn.

Row 3: 1 ch (does NOT count as st), 1 dc into first dc, *1 ch, miss 4 sts, (1 dtr, 1 ch, 1 dtr, 1 ch, 1 dtr, 1 ch, 1 dtr, 1 ch and 1 dtr) all into next st, 1 ch, miss 4 sts, 1 dc into next st, rep from * to end.

Fasten off.

Mark positions for 6 buttons along this band - lowest button 20 cm up from lower edge, top button 1.5 cm down from neck edge, and rem 4 buttons evenly spaced between.

Buttonhole band

Work to match button band, working buttonholes in row 2 to correspond with positions marked for buttons on button band by replacing (1 dc into each of next 3 dc) with (3 ch, miss 3 dc).

Cuff edging

With RS facing and using 2.50mm (US C2) hook, attach yarn to one end of foundation ch edge of sleeve and work across foundation ch edge as folls:

Row 1 (RS): 1 ch (does NOT count as st), work in dc evenly to end, ensuring number of dc worked is a multiple of 10 plus one extra, turn.

Row 2: 1 ch (does NOT count as st), 1 dc into each dc to end, turn.

Row 3: 5 ch (counts as 1 dtr and 1 ch), (1 dtr, 1 ch and 1 dtr) into dc at base of 5 ch, ★1 ch, miss 4 dc, 1 dc into next dc, 1 ch, miss 4 dc★★, (1 dtr, 1 ch, 1 dtr, 1 ch, 1 dtr, 1 ch, 1 dtr, 1 ch and 1 dtr) all into next dc, rep from ★ to end, ending last rep at ★★, (1 dtr, 1 ch, 1 dtr, 1 ch and 1 dtr) all into last dc, turn.

Row 4: 1 ch (does NOT count as st), 1 dc into first dtr, ★2 ch, miss 5 sts, (1 ttr, 2 ch, 1 ttr, 2 ch, 1 ttr, 2 ch and 1 ttr) into next dc, 2 ch, miss 5 sts, 1 dc into next dtr, rep from ★ to end, working dc at end of last rep into 4th of 5 ch at beg of previous row, turn.

Row 5: 1 ch (does NOT count as st), 1 dc into first dc, ★4 ch, miss (2 ch and 1 ttr), (tr3tog into next ch sp, 3 ch, miss 1 ttr) twice, tr3tog into next ch sp, 4 ch, miss (1 ttr and 2 ch), 1 dc into next dc, rep from ★ to end.

Fasten off.

Collar edging

Working across foundation ch edge of collar, work as given for cuff edging to end of row 4.

Fasten off.

Row 5 (RS): Rejoin yarn at marker nearest fasten-off point, 1 ch (does NOT count as st), work in dc along row-end edge of collar and edging to dc at end of edging row 4, work 1 dc into last dc of row 4, ★4 ch, miss (2 ch and 1 ttr), (tr3tog into next ch sp, 3 ch, miss 1 ttr) twice, tr3tog into next ch sp, 4 ch, miss (1 ttr and 2 ch), 1 dc into next dc, rep from ★ to end, now work in dc along other row-end edge of edging and collar to other marker.

Fasten off.

Positioning markers level with first row of bands, sew shaped edge of collar to neck edge, easing in fullness.

See information page for finishing instructions, setting in sleeves using the set-in method.

Hem edging

Work as given for cuff edging, working across foundation ch edges of fronts and back and beg and ending at ends of row 3 of bands.

Belt

Using 2.50mm (US C2) hook make 11 ch.

Row 1 (RS): 1 dc into 2nd ch from hook, 1 dc into each ch to end, turn. 10 sts.

Row 2: 1 ch (does NOT count as st), 1 dc into each dc to end, turn.

Rep last row until belt meas 130 [140: 150: 160: 170] cm.

Fasten off.

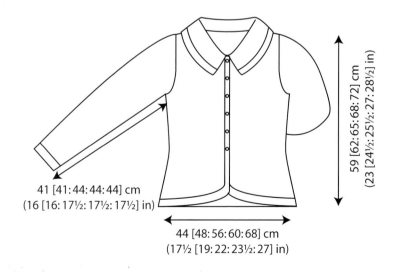

41 [41: 44: 44: 44] cm
(16 [16: 17½: 17½: 17½] in)

44 [48: 56: 60: 68] cm
(17½ [19: 22: 23½: 27] in)

59 [62: 65: 68: 72] cm
(23 [24½: 25½: 27: 28½] in)

Main Image Page 12

Banana Wrap ❋❋
By Marie Wallin

YARN
Rowan Panama

    9   x 50gm

(photographed in Begonia 306)

NEEDLES
1 pair 3¼mm (no 10) (US 3) needles

3¼mm (no 10) (US 3) circular needle, 100 cm long

TENSION
26 sts and 39 rows to 10 cm measured over patt using 3¼mm (US 3) needles.

FINISHED SIZE
Completed shawl measures 203 cm (80 ins) at widest point and is 68 cm (27 ins) deep.

SHAWL

Using 3¼mm (US 3) circular needle cast on 527 sts.

Row 1 (WS): Purl.

Now work in patt and shape sides as folls:

Row 1 (RS): Sl 1, K1, psso, ★K1, yfwd, sl 1, K1, psso, K2, yfwd, sl 1, K1, psso, K1, yfwd, sl 1, K2tog, psso, yfwd, K1, K2tog, yfwd, K2, K2tog, yfwd, rep from ★ to last 3 sts, K1, K2tog.

Row 2: P2tog, P1, ★yrn, P2tog, P2, yrn, P2tog, P3, P2tog tbl, yrn, P2, P2tog tbl, yrn, P3, rep from ★ to last 18 sts, yrn, P2tog, P2, yrn, P2tog, P3, P2tog tbl, yrn, P2, P2tog tbl, yrn, P1, P2tog tbl.

Row 3: Sl 1, K1, psso, K1, yfwd, sl 1, K1, psso, K2, yfwd, sl 1, K1, psso, K1, K2tog, yfwd, K2, K2tog, yfwd, ★K5, yfwd, sl 1, K1, psso, K2, yfwd, sl 1, K1, psso, K1, K2tog, yfwd, K2, K2tog, yfwd, rep from ★ to last 3 sts, K1, K2tog.

Row 4: P2tog, P1, ★yrn, P2tog, P2, yrn, P3tog, yrn, P2, P2tog tbl, yrn, P7, rep from ★ to last 14 sts, yrn, P2tog, P2, yrn, P3tog, yrn, P2, P2tog tbl, yrn, P1, P2tog tbl.

Row 5: Sl 1, K1, psso, K1, yfwd, sl 1, K1, psso, K5, K2tog, yfwd, ★K2, K2tog, yfwd, K1, yfwd, sl 1, K1, psso, K2, yfwd, sl 1, K1, psso, K2, yfwd, sl 1, K1, psso, K5, K2tog, yfwd, rep from ★ to last 3 sts, K1, K2tog.

Row 6: P2tog, P1, ★yrn, P2tog, P3, P2tog tbl, yrn, P2, P2tog tbl, yrn, P3, yrn, P2tog, P2, rep from ★ to last 10 sts, yrn, P2tog, P3, P2tog tbl, yrn, P1, P2tog tbl.

Row 7: Sl 1, K1, psso, K1, yfwd, sl 1, K1, psso, K1, K2tog, yfwd, ★K2, K2tog, yfwd, K5, yfwd, sl 1, K1, psso, K2, yfwd, sl 1, K1, psso, K1, K2tog, yfwd, rep from ★ to last 3 sts, K1, K2tog.

Row 8: P2tog, P1, ★yrn, P3tog, yrn, P2, P2tog tbl, yrn, P2, yrn, P3tog, yrn, P2, yrn, P2tog, P2, rep from ★ to last 6 sts, yrn, P3tog, yrn, P1, P2tog tbl.

Row 9: Sl 1, K1, psso, K to last 2 sts, K2tog. 509 sts.

Row 10: P2tog, P1, ★yrn, P2tog, P2, yrn, P2tog, P1, yrn, P3tog, yrn, P1, P2tog tbl, yrn, P2, P2tog tbl, yrn, P1, rep from ★ to last 2 sts, P2tog tbl.

Row 11: Sl 1, K1, psso, K1, yfwd, sl 1, K1, psso, K2, yfwd, sl 1, K1, psso, K3, K2tog, yfwd, K2, K2tog, yfwd, ★K3, yfwd, sl 1, K1, psso, K2, yfwd, sl 1, K1, psso, K3, K2tog, yfwd, K2, K2tog, yfwd, rep from ★ to last 3 sts, K1, K2tog.

Row 12: P2tog, P1, ★yrn, P2tog, P2, yrn, P2tog, P1, P2tog tbl, yrn, P2, P2tog tbl, yrn, P5, rep from ★ to last 16 sts, yrn, P2tog, P2, yrn, P2tog, P1, P2tog tbl, yrn, P2, yrn, P2tog tbl, yrn, P1, P2tog tbl.

Row 13: Sl 1, K1, psso, K1, yfwd, sl 1, K1, psso, K2, yfwd, sl 1, K2tog, psso, yfwd, K2, K2tog, yfwd, ★K7, yfwd, sl 1, K1, psso, K2, yfwd, sl 1, K2tog, psso, yfwd, K2, K2tog, yfwd, rep from ★ to last 3 sts, K1, K2tog.

Row 14: P2tog, P1, ★yrn, P2tog, P5, P2tog tbl, yrn, P2, P2tog tbl, yrn, P1, yrn, P2tog, P2, rep from ★ to last 12 sts, yrn, P2tog, P5, P2tog tbl, yrn, P1, P2tog tbl.

Row 15: Sl 1, K1, psso, K1, yfwd, sl 1, K1, psso, K3, K2tog, yfwd, ★K2, K2tog, yfwd, K3, yfwd, sl 1, K1, psso, K2, yfwd, sl 1, K1, psso, K3, K2tog, yfwd, rep from ★ to last 3 sts, K1, K2tog.

Row 16: P2tog, P1, ★yrn, P2tog, P1, P2tog tbl, yrn, P2, P2tog tbl, yrn, P5, yrn, P2tog, P2, rep from ★ to last 8 sts, yrn, P2tog, P1, P2tog tbl, yrn, P1, P2tog tbl.

Row 17: Sl 1, K1, psso, K1, yfwd, sl 1, K2tog, psso, yfwd, ★K2, K2tog, yfwd, K2, yfwd, sl 1, K2tog, psso, yfwd, K2, yfwd, sl 1, K1, psso, K2, yfwd, sl 1, K2tog, psso, yfwd, rep from ★ to last 3 sts, K1, K2tog.

Row 18: P2tog, P to last 2 sts, P2tog tbl. 491 sts.

Rep rows 1 to 18, 13 times more. 23 sts. (**Note:** Change to straight needles when there are few enough sts to fit comfortably onto straight needles.)

Now complete point as folls:

Row 1 (RS): Sl 1, K1, psso, K1, yfwd, sl 1, K1, psso, K2, yfwd, sl 1, K1, psso, K1, yfwd, sl 1, K2tog, psso, yfwd, K1, K2tog, yfwd, K2, K2tog, yfwd, K1, K2tog.

Row 2: P2tog, P1, yrn, P2tog, P2, yrn, P2tog, P3, P2tog tbl, yrn, P2,

P2tog tbl, yrn, P1, P2tog tbl.

Row 3: Sl 1, K1, psso, K1, yfwd, sl 1, K1, psso, K2, yfwd, sl 1, K1, psso, K1, K2tog, yfwd, K2, K2tog, yfwd, K1, K2tog.

Row 4: P2tog, P1, yrn, P2tog, P2, yrn, P3tog, yrn, P2, P2tog tbl, yrn, P1, P2tog tbl.

Row 5: Sl 1, K1, psso, K1, yfwd, sl 1, K1, psso, K5, K2tog, yfwd, K1, K2tog.

Row 6: P2tog, P1, yrn, P2tog, P3, P2tog tbl, yrn, P1, P2tog tbl.

Row 7: Sl 1, K1, psso, K1, yfwd, sl 1, K1, psso, K1, K2tog, yfwd, K1, K2tog.

Row 8: P2tog, P1, yrn, P3tog, yrn, P1, P2tog tbl.

Row 9: Sl 1, K1, psso, K3, K2tog.

Row 10: P2tog, P1, P2tog tbl.

Row 11: Sl 1, K2tog, psso and fasten off.

MAKING UP
Press as described on the information page.

Bread Fruit ❋❋
By Lisa Richardson

Main Image Page 32

SIZE

	S	M	L	XL	XXL	
To fit bust						
	81-86	91-97	102-107	112-117	122-127	cm
	32-34	36-38	40-42	44-46	48-50	in

YARN
Rowan Panama

9	10	11	12	13	x 50gm

(photographed in Aster 310)

CROCHET HOOKS
3.00mm (no 11) (US C2) crochet hook

TENSION
21½ sts and 15 rows to 10 cm measured over patt using 3.00mm (US C2) crochet hook.

CROCHET ABBREVIATIONS
ch = chain; **ss** = slip stitch; **dc** = double crochet; **tr** = treble; **dtr** = double treble; **sp(s)** = space(s).

BACK
Using 3.00mm (US C2) hook make 100 [107: 121: 135: 142] ch.

Row 1 (RS): 1 dc into 2nd ch from hook, 1 dc into each ch to end, turn. 99 [106: 120: 134: 141] sts.

Row 2: 1 ch (does NOT count as st), 1 dc into each dc to end, turn. This row forms dc fabric.

Cont in dc fabric until back meas 7 cm, ending with RS facing for next row.

Next row (RS): 1 ch (does NOT count as st), 1 dc into each of first 3 dc, ★5 ch, miss 2 dc★★, 1 dc into each of next 5 dc, rep from ★ to end, ending last rep at ★★, 1 dc into each of last 3 dc, turn. 14 [15: 17: 19: 20] patt reps.

Now work in patt as folls:

Row 1 (WS): 1 ch (does NOT count as st), 1 dc into each of first 2 dc,

*3 ch, miss 1 dc, 1 dc into next ch sp, 3 ch, miss 1 dc**, 1 dc into each of next 3 dc, rep from * to end, ending last rep at **, 1 dc into each of last 2 dc, turn.

Row 2: 1 ch (does NOT count as st), 1 dc into first dc, *3 ch, miss 1 dc, 1 dc into next ch sp, 1 dc into next dc, 1 dc into next ch sp, 3 ch, miss 1 dc, 1 dc into next dc, rep from * to end, turn.

Row 3: 5 ch (counts as 1 tr and 2 ch), miss first dc, *1 dc into next ch sp, 1 dc into each of next 3 dc, 1 dc into next ch sp**, 5 ch, miss 1 dc, rep from * to end, ending last rep at **, 2 ch, 1 tr into last dc, turn.

Row 4: 1 ch (does NOT count as st), 1 dc into tr at end of previous row, *3 ch, miss 1 dc, 1 dc into each of next 3 dc, 3 ch, miss 1 dc, 1 dc into next ch sp, rep from * to end, working dc at end of last rep into 3rd of 5 ch at beg of previous row, turn.

Row 5: 1 ch (does NOT count as st), 1 dc into first dc, *1 dc into next ch sp, 3 ch, miss 1 dc, 1 dc into next dc, 3 ch, miss 1 dc, 1 dc into next ch sp, 1 dc into next dc, rep from * to end, turn.

Row 6: 1 ch (does NOT count as st), 1 dc into each of first 2 dc, *1 dc into next ch sp, 5 ch, miss 1 dc, 1 dc into next ch sp**, 1 dc into each of next 3 dc, rep from * to end, ending last rep at **, 1 dc into each of last 2 dc, turn.

These 6 rows form patt.

Cont in patt until back meas approx 34 [34: 34: 38: 38] cm, ending after patt row 4 and with **WS** facing for next row.

Shape for cap sleeves

Row 1 (WS): 1 ch (does NOT count as st), 2 dc into first dc, 1 dc into next ch sp, patt until dc has been worked in last ch sp, 2 dc into last dc, turn.

Row 2: 1 ch (does NOT count as st), 2 dc into first dc, 1 dc into each of next 2 dc, 1 dc into next ch sp, patt until dc has been worked into last ch sp, 1 dc into each of next 2 dc, 2 dc into last dc, turn.

Row 3: 4 ch, 1 dc into 2nd ch from hook, 3 ch, miss 1 dc, 1 dc into each of next 3 dc, patt until the 3 dc have been worked into centre 3 dc of last 5-dc group, 3 ch, 1 dtr into last dc, turn. 15 [16: 18: 20: 21] patt reps.

Row 4: 1 ch (does NOT count as st), 2 dc into first dtr, 1 dc into next ch sp, patt until dc has been worked in last ch sp, 2 dc into last dc, turn.

Rows 5 and 6: As rows 2 and 3. 16 [17: 19: 21: 22] patt reps.

Row 7: As row 4.

Rows 8 and 9: As rows 2 and 3. 17 [18: 20: 22: 23] patt reps.

Place markers at both ends of last row to denote base of armhole openings.

Cont straight until armhole meas approx 20 [21: 22: 23: 24] cm, ending when **centre** patt rep consists of "1 dc into next ch sp, 1 dc into next dc, 1 dc into next ch sp".

Shape back neck

Place marker on centre st of centre patt rep, then place markers on 4th patt rep either side of centre marker – 8 patt reps between outer markers. Remove centre marker.

Next row: Patt until (1 dc into next ch sp, 1 dc into each of next 3 dc, 1 dc into next ch sp) has been worked over first marked patt rep, (3 ch, miss 1 dc, 1 dc into next ch sp, 1 dc into each of next 3 dc, 1 dc into next ch sp) 8 times, patt to end, turn.

Next row: Patt until 3 dc have been worked into centre 3 dc of the 5 dc of first marked patt rep and turn, leaving rem sts unworked. Work on this set of sts only for first side of neck.

Next row: 1 ch (does NOT count as st), miss first dc, 1 dc into next dc, 3 ch, 1 dc into next ch sp, patt to end of row, turn.

Next row: Patt until 1 dc has been worked into each of last group of 3 dc, 1 dc into next ch sp, turn.

Next row: 1 ch (does NOT count as st), miss first dc, 1 dc into each of next 3 dc, patt to end, turn.

Next row: Patt until dc has been worked into centre dc of last group of 3 dc, turn.

Next row: 1 ss into first dc and next 2 ch, 1 ch (does NOT count as st), 1 dc into ch sp at base of 1 ch, 1 dc into each of next 3 dc, 1 dc into next ch sp, patt to end.

Fasten off.

Return to last complete row worked, miss centre (3 ch and 5 dc) 7 times, next 3 ch and foll dc, attach yarn to next dc and cont as folls:

Next row: 1 ch (does NOT count as st), 1 dc into dc where yarn was rejoined, 1 dc into each of next 2 dc, patt to end, turn.

Next row: Patt until dc has been worked into centre dc of last group of 3 dc, turn.

Next row: 1 ss into first dc and next 2 ch, 1 ch (does NOT count as st), 1 dc into ch sp at base of 1 ch, 1 dc into each of next 3 dc, 1 dc into next ch sp, patt to end, turn.

Next row: Patt until 3 dc have been worked into centre 3 dc of last 5 dc group, turn.

Next row: 1 ch (does NOT count as st), miss first dc, 1 dc into next dc, 3 ch, 1 dc into next ch sp, patt to end of row, turn.

Next row: Patt until 1 dc has been worked into each of last group of 3 dc, 1 dc into next ch sp.

Fasten off.

FRONT

Work as given for back until 6 rows less have been worked than on back to beg of back neck shaping, ending when **centre** patt rep consists of "1 dc into next ch sp, 1 dc into next dc, 1 dc into next ch sp".

Shape front neck

Place marker on centre st of centre patt rep, then place markers on 3rd patt rep either side of centre marker – 6 patt reps between outer markers. Remove centre marker.

Next row: Patt until (1 dc into next ch sp, 1 dc into each of next 3 dc, 1 dc into next ch sp) has been worked over first marked patt rep, (3 ch, miss 1 dc, 1 dc into next ch sp, 1 dc into each of next 3 dc, 1 dc into next ch sp) 8 times, patt to end, turn.

Next row: Patt until 3 dc have been worked into centre 3 dc of the 5 dc of first marked patt rep and turn, leaving rem sts unworked. Work on this set of sts only for first side of neck.

***Next row**: 1 ch (does NOT count as st), miss first dc, 1 dc into next dc, 3 ch, 1 dc into next ch sp, patt to end of row, turn.

Next row: Patt until 1 dc has been worked into each of last group of 3 dc, 1 dc into next ch sp, turn.

Next row: 1 ch (does NOT count as st), miss first dc, 1 dc into each of next 3 dc, patt to end, turn.

Next row: Patt until dc has been worked into centre dc of last group of 3 dc, turn.

Next row: 1 ss into first dc and next 2 ch, 1 ch (does NOT count as st), 1 dc into ch sp at base of 1 ch, 1 dc into each of next 3 dc, 1 dc into next ch sp, patt to end, turn.★★★

Next row: Patt until 3 dc have been worked into centre 3 dc of last 5 dc group, turn.

Rep from ★★★ to ★★★ once more.

Fasten off.

Return to last complete row worked, miss centre (3 ch and 5 dc) 5 times, next 3 ch and foll dc, attach yarn to next dc and cont as folls:

Next row: 1 ch (does NOT count as st), 1 dc into dc where yarn was rejoined, 1 dc into each of next 2 dc, patt to end, turn.

Complete to match first side, reversing shapings by working shaping as given for second side of back neck.

MAKING UP

Press as described on the information page.

Join both shoulder seams.

Neckband

With RS facing and using 3.00mm (US C2) hook, attach yarn at neck edge of one shoulder seam, 1 ch (does NOT count as st), work 1 round of dc evenly around entire neck edge, ss to first dc, turn.

Next round: 1 ch (does NOT count as st), 1 dc into each dc to end, ss to first dc, turn.

Rep last round once more.

Fasten off.

Join side seams below markers.

Cuffs (both alike)

With RS facing and using 3.00mm (US C2) hook, attach yarn at top of side seam, 1 ch (does NOT count as st), work 1 round of dc evenly around entire armhole edge, ss to first dc, turn.

Next round: 1 ch (does NOT count as st), 1 dc into each dc to end, ss to first dc, turn.

Rep last round until cuff meas 13 cm.

Fasten off.

See information page for finishing instructions.

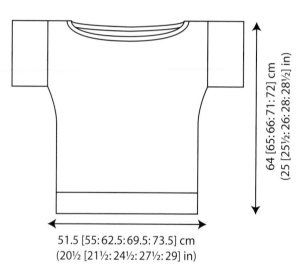

64 [65:66:71:72] cm
(25 [25½:26:28:28½] in)

51.5 [55:62.5:69.5:73.5] cm
(20½ [21½:24½:27½:29] in)

Main Image Page 18

Candlenut ✳✳
By Grace Melville

SIZE

	S	M	L	XL	XXL	
To fit bust						
	81-86	91-97	102-107	112-117	122-127	cm
	32-34	36-38	40-42	44-46	48-50	in

YARN

Rowan Panama

5	5	6	7	8	x 50gm

(photographed in Morning Glory 302)

NEEDLES

1 pair 2¾mm (no 12) (US 2) needles
1 pair 3¼mm (no 10) (US 3) needles

TENSION

24 sts and 32 rows to 10 cm measured over patt using 3¼mm (US 3) needles.

BACK

Using 2¾mm (US 2) needles cast on 136 [149: 163: 183: 203] sts.
Work in g st for 7 rows, ending with **WS** facing for next row.
Change to 3¼mm (US 3) needles.
Row 8 (WS): P4 [6: 4: 5: 6], P2tog, (P7, P2tog) 14 [15: 17: 19: 21] times, P4 [6: 4: 5: 6]. 121 [133: 145: 163: 181] sts.
Now work in patt as folls:
Row 1 (RS): K2tog, yfwd, K3, ★yfwd, sl 1, K2tog, psso, yfwd, K3, rep from ★ to last 2 sts, yfwd, sl 1, K1, psso.
Row 2: P1, ★yrn, P2tog, P1, P2tog tbl, yrn, P1, rep from ★ to end.
Row 3: ★K2, yfwd, sl 1, K2tog, psso, yfwd, K1, rep from ★ to last st, K1.
Row 4: P1, ★P2tog tbl, yrn, P1, yrn, P2tog, P1, rep from ★ to end.
These 4 rows form patt.
Cont in patt until back meas 38 [40: 42: 44: 46] cm, ending with RS facing for next row.

Shape back neck and shoulders

Next row (RS): Cast off 11 [13: 14: 17: 20] sts, patt until there are 29 [33: 37: 43: 48] sts on right needle and turn, leaving rem sts on a holder.
Work each side of neck separately.
Cast off 5 sts at beg of next row, 11 [13: 14: 17: 20] sts at beg of foll row, then 3 sts at beg of next row.
Cast off rem 10 [12: 15: 18: 20] sts.
With RS facing, rejoin yarn to rem sts, cast off centre 41 [41: 43: 43: 45] sts, patt to end.
Complete to match first side, reversing shapings.

FRONT

Work as given for back until 14 [14: 16: 16: 18] rows less have been worked than on back to beg of shoulder shaping, ending with RS facing for next row.

Shape front neck

Next row (RS): Patt 42 [48: 54: 63: 72] sts and turn, leaving rem sts on a holder.
Work each side of neck separately.
Keeping patt correct, dec 1 st at neck edge of next 8 rows, then on foll 2 [2: 3: 3: 4] alt rows. 32 [38: 43: 52: 60] sts.
Work 1 row, ending with RS facing for next row.

Shape shoulder

Cast off 11 [13: 14: 17: 20] sts at beg of next and foll alt row.
Work 1 row.
Cast off rem 10 [12: 15: 18: 20] sts.
With RS facing, rejoin yarn to rem sts, cast off centre 37 sts, patt to end.
Complete to match first side, reversing shapings.

MAKING UP

Press as described on the information page.
Join right shoulder seam using back stitch, or mattress stitch if preferred.

Neckband

With RS facing and using 2¾mm (US 2) needles, pick up and knit 14 [14: 16: 16: 18] sts down left side of neck, 41 sts from front, 14 [14: 16: 16: 18] sts up right side of neck, then 63 [63: 65: 65: 67] sts from back. 132 [132: 138: 138: 144] sts.
Work in g st for 6 rows, ending with **WS** facing for next row.
Cast off knitwise (on **WS**).
Join left shoulder and neckband seam.

Side borders (both alike)

With RS facing and using 2¾mm (US 2) needles, pick up and knit 103 [108: 113: 119: 124] sts evenly up one row-end edge from cast-on edge to shoulder seam, then 103 [108: 113: 119: 124] sts evenly down next row-end edge to cast-on edge. 206 [216: 226: 238: 248] sts.

Work in g st for 6 rows, ending with **WS** facing for next row.
Cast off knitwise (on **WS**).
Ties (make 4)
Using 2 3/4mm (US 2) needles cast on 5 sts.
Work in g st for 30 cm, ending with **WS** facing for next row.
Cast off knitwise (on **WS**).
Mark points along side seam edges of back and front 22 [23: 24: 25: 26] cm down from shoulder seams, then sew cast-on edge of ties to cast-off edges of side borders at these points.
See information page for finishing instructions.

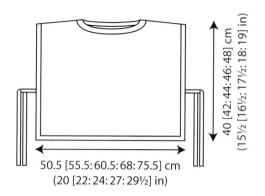

50.5 [55.5: 60.5: 68: 75.5] cm
(20 [22: 24: 27: 29½] in)

40 [42: 44: 46: 48] cm
(15½ [16½: 17½: 18: 19] in)

Carob ✤✤
By Marie Wallin

Main Image Page 28

SIZE

	S	M	L	XL	XXL	
To fit bust						
	81-86	91-97	102-107	112-117	122-127	cm
	32-34	36-38	40-42	44-46	48-50	in

YARN

Rowan Panama

A Nightshade 312

	5	5	6	6	7	x 50gm

B Begonia 306

	3	3	4	4	4	x 50gm

C Hibiscus 311

	2	3	3	3	3	x 50gm

D Tulip 307

	2	2	2	2	2	x 50gm

NEEDLES

1 pair 2¾mm (no 12) (US 2) needles
1 pair 3¼mm (no 10) (US 3) needles

BUTTONS - 4 x RW5019 from Bedecked. See information page for

contact details.

TENSION

27 sts and 36 rows to 10 cm measured over st st, 27 sts and 43 rows to 10 cm measured over moss st, both using 3¼mm (US 3) needles. 30 sts and 58 rows to 10 cm measured over g st using 2¾mm (US 2) needles.

BACK

Hemband

Using 2¾mm (US 2) needles and yarn A cast on 25 sts.
Work in g st as folls:
Work 4 rows, ending with RS facing for next row.
Row 5 (RS): K18, wrap next st (by slipping next st on left needle onto right needle, taking yarn to opposite side of work between needles and then slipping same st back onto left needle - when working back across wrapped sts, work the wrapped st and the wrapping loop tog as one st) and turn.
Row 6: Knit.
Row 7: K13, wrap next st and turn.
Row 8: Knit.
Row 9: K8, wrap next st and turn.
Row 10: Knit.

Cont straight until **longer** row-end edge meas 46 [51: 57: 63: 70] cm, ending with RS facing for next row.

Next row (RS): K8, wrap next st and turn.

Next row: Knit.

Next row: K13, wrap next st and turn.

Next row: Knit.

Next row: K18, wrap next st and turn.

Next row: Knit.

Work 4 rows across all sts, ending with RS facing for next row.

Cast off.

Main section

With RS facing, using 3¼ mm (US 3) needles and yarn B, pick up and knit 121 [135: 151: 167: 185] sts evenly along **shorter** row-end edge of hemband.

Beg with a P row, work in st st as folls:

Dec 1 st at each end of 4th and 4 foll 4th rows. 111 [125: 141: 157: 175] sts.

Work 15 [19: 19: 19: 19] rows, ending with RS facing for next row.

Inc 1 st at each end of next row. 113 [127: 143: 159: 177] sts.

Work 3 rows, ending with RS facing for next row.

Break off yarn B and join in yarn C.

Next row (RS): Knit.

Now work in moss st as folls:

Row 1: K1, ★P1, K1, rep from ★ to end.

Row 2: As row 1.

These 2 rows form moss st.

Cont in moss st, inc 1 st at each end of 10th [10th: 12th: 14th: 14th] and 1 [1: 0: 0: 0] foll 16th row. 117 [131: 145: 161: 179] sts.

Work 1 [1: 17: 17: 17] rows, ending with RS facing for next row.

Break off yarn C and join in yarn D.

Beg with a K row, work in st st, inc 1 st at each end of 15th [15th: 3rd: 3rd: 3rd] and foll - [-: 18th: 18th: 20th] row. 119 [133: 149: 165: 183] sts.

Work 3 [3: 1: 1: 3] rows, ending with RS facing for next row.

Break off yarn D and join in yarn A.

Next row (RS): Knit.

Now work in moss st as folls:

Work 11 rows, ending with RS facing for next row. (Back should meas 34 [35: 36: 37: 38] cm.)

Shape armholes

Keeping moss st correct, cast off 6 [7: 8: 9: 10] sts at beg of next 2 rows. 107 [119: 133: 147: 163] sts.

Dec 1 st at each end of next 7 [7: 9: 9: 11] rows, then on foll 3 [7: 8: 10: 12] alt rows. 87 [91: 99: 109: 117] sts.

Work 15 [11: 11: 13: 11] rows, ending with RS facing for next row.

Break off yarn A and join in yarn B.

Beg with a K row, work in st st for 28 rows, ending with RS facing for next row.

Break off yarn B and join in yarn C.

Next row (RS): Knit.

Now work in moss st as folls:

Work 21 rows, ending with RS facing for next row. (Armhole should meas 20 [21: 22: 23: 24] cm.)

Shape shoulders and back neck

Next row (RS): Cast off 4 [5: 6: 7: 8] sts, moss st until there are 21 [22: 24: 28: 30] sts on right needle and turn, leaving rem sts on a holder.

Work each side of neck separately.

Cast off 3 sts at beg of next row, 4 [5: 5: 7: 7] sts at beg of foll row, 3 sts at beg of next row, 4 [4: 5: 6: 7] sts at beg of foll row, then 3 sts at beg of next row.

Cast off rem 4 [4: 5: 6: 7] sts.

With RS facing, rejoin yarn to rem sts, cast off centre 37 [37: 39: 39: 41] sts, moss st to end.

Complete to match first side, reversing shapings.

LEFT FRONT

Hemband

Using 2¾ mm (US 2) needles and yarn A cast on 25 sts.

Work in g st until hemband meas 21 [23.5: 26.5: 29.5: 33] cm, ending with RS facing for next row.

Next row (RS): K8, wrap next st and turn.

Next row: Knit.

Next row: K13, wrap next st and turn.

Next row: Knit.

Next row: K18, wrap next st and turn.

Next row: Knit.

Work 4 rows across all sts, ending with RS facing for next row.

Cast off.

Main section

With RS facing, using 3¼ mm (US 3) needles and yarn B, pick up and knit 58 [65: 73: 81: 90] sts evenly along **shorter** row-end edge of hemband.

Beg with a P row, work in st st as folls:

Dec 1 st at beg of 4th and 4 foll 4th rows. 53 [60: 68: 76: 85] sts.

Work 15 [19: 19: 19: 19] rows, ending with RS facing for next row.

Inc 1 st at beg of next row. 54 [61: 69: 77: 86] sts.

Work 3 rows, ending with RS facing for next row.

Break off yarn B and join in yarn C.

Next row (RS): Knit.

Now work in moss st as folls:

Row 1: K0 [1: 1: 1: 0], ★P1, K1, rep from ★ to end.

Row 2: ★K1, P1, rep from ★ to last 0 [1: 1: 1: 0] st, K0 [1: 1: 1: 0].

These 2 rows form moss st.

Cont in moss st, inc 1 st at beg of 10th [10th: 12th: 14th: 14th] and 1 [1: 0: 0: 0] foll 16th row. 56 [63: 70: 78: 87] sts.

Work 1 [1: 17: 17: 17] rows, ending with RS facing for next row.

Break off yarn C and join in yarn D.

Beg with a K row, work in st st, inc 1 st at beg of 15th [15th: 3rd: 3rd: 3rd] and foll - [-: 18th: 18th: 20th] row. 57 [64: 72: 80: 89] sts.

Work 3 [3: 1: 1: 3] rows, ending with RS facing for next row.

Break off yarn D and join in yarn A.

Next row (RS): Knit.

Now work in moss st as folls:

Work 11 rows, ending with RS facing for next row.

Shape armhole

Keeping moss st correct, cast off 6 [7: 8: 9: 10] sts at beg of next row. 51 [57: 64: 71: 79] sts.

Work 1 row.

Dec 1 st at armhole edge of next 7 [7: 9: 9: 11] rows, then on foll 3 [7: 8: 10: 12] alt rows. 41 [43: 47: 52: 56] sts.

Work 15 [11: 11: 13: 11] rows, ending with RS facing for next row.

Break off yarn A and join in yarn B.

Beg with a K row, work in st st for 15 [15: 11: 11: 7] rows, ending with **WS** facing for next row.

Shape front neck

Cast off 11 sts at beg of next row. 30 [32: 36: 41: 45] sts.

Dec 1 st at neck edge of next 9 rows, then on foll alt row, then on 0 [0: 1: 1: 2] foll 4th rows. 20 [22: 25: 30: 33] sts.

Work 1 row, ending with RS facing for next row.

Break off yarn B and join in yarn C.

Next row (RS): Knit.

Now work in moss st as set by previous bands as folls:

Dec 1 st at neck edge of 2nd and foll 4th row, then on 2 foll 6th rows. 16 [18: 21: 26: 29] sts.

Work 3 rows, ending with RS facing for next row.

Shape shoulder

Cast off 4 [5: 6: 7: 8] sts at beg of next and foll 2 [1: 0: 1: 0] alt rows, then 0 [4: 5: 6: 7] sts at beg of foll 0 [1: 2: 1: 2] alt rows.

Work 1 row.

Cast off rem 4 [4: 5: 6: 7] sts.

RIGHT FRONT

Hemband

Using 2¾mm (US 2) needles and yarn A cast on 25 sts.

Work in g st as folls:

Work 4 rows, ending with RS facing for next row.

Row 5 (RS): K18, wrap next st and turn.

Row 6: Knit.

Row 7: K13, wrap next st and turn.

Row 8: Knit.

Row 9: K8, wrap next st and turn.

Row 10: Knit.

Cont straight until **longer** row-end edge meas 23 [25.5: 28.5: 31.5: 35] cm, ending with RS facing for next row.

Cast off.

Main section

With RS facing, using 3¼mm (US 3) needles and yarn B, pick up and knit 58 [65: 73: 81: 90] sts evenly along **shorter** row-end edge of hemband.

Beg with a P row, work in st st as folls:

Dec 1 st at end of 4th and 4 foll 4th rows. 53 [60: 68: 76: 85] sts.

Work 15 [19: 19: 19: 19] rows, ending with RS facing for next row.

Inc 1 st at end of next row. 54 [61: 69: 77: 86] sts.

Work 3 rows, ending with RS facing for next row.

Break off yarn B and join in yarn C.

Next row (RS): Knit.

Now work in moss st as folls:

Row 1: ★K1, P1, rep from ★ to last 0 [1: 1: 1: 0] st, K0 [1: 1: 1: 0].

Row 2: K0 [1: 1: 1: 0], ★P1, K1, rep from ★ to end.

These 2 rows form moss st.

Complete to match left front, reversing shapings.

SLEEVES

Cuff band

Using 2¾mm (US 2) needles and yarn A cast on 36 sts.

Work in g st as folls:

Work 4 rows, ending with RS facing for next row.

Row 5 (RS): K27, wrap next st and turn.

Row 6: Knit.

Row 7: K18, wrap next st and turn.

Row 8: Knit.

Row 9: K9, wrap next st and turn.

Row 10: Knit.

Cont straight until **shorter** row-end edge meas 19 [20: 21: 21: 22] cm, ending with RS facing for next row.

Next row (RS): K9, wrap next st and turn.

Next row: Knit.

Next row: K18, wrap next st and turn.

Next row: Knit.

Next row: K27, wrap next st and turn.

Next row: Knit.

Work 4 rows across all sts, ending with RS facing for next row.

Cast off.

Main section

With RS facing, using 3¼mm (US 3) needles and yarn B, pick up and knit 61 [63: 65: 65: 67] sts evenly along **longer** row-end edge of cuff band.

Beg with a P row, work in st st as folls:

Inc 1 st at each end of 2nd and 11 [12: 13: 12: 11] foll 4th rows, then on 1 [1: 0: 0: 0] foll 6th row. 87 [91: 93: 91: 91] sts.

Work 1 [1: 3: 3: 3] rows, ending with RS facing for next row.

Break off yarn B and join in yarn C.

Next row (RS): (Inc in first st) 0 [0: 0: 1: 1] times, K to last 0 [0: 0: 1: 1] st, (inc in last st) 0 [0: 0: 1: 1] times. 87 [91: 93: 93: 93] sts.

Now work in moss st as given for back, inc 1 st at each end of 4th [4th: 2nd: 4th: 4th] and 0 [0: 0: 5: 7] foll 4th rows, then on 4 [4: 4: 1: 0] foll 6th rows. 97 [101: 103: 107: 109] sts.

Work 1 [1: 3: 3: 1] rows, ending with RS facing for next row.

Break off yarn C and join in yarn D.

Beg with a K row, work in st st, inc 1 st at each end of 5th [5th: 3rd: 3rd: 3rd] and 0 [0: 0: 0: 1] foll 4th row, then on 2 [2: 3: 3: 3] foll 6th rows. 103 [107: 111: 115: 119] sts.

Work 1 row, ending with RS facing for next row.

Break off yarn D and join in yarn A.

Next row (RS): Knit.

Now work in moss st for 11 rows, ending with RS facing for next row. (Sleeve should meas 42 [43: 44: 44: 44] cm.)

Shape top

Keeping moss st correct, cast off 6 [7: 8: 9: 10] sts at beg of next 2 rows. 91 [93: 95: 97: 99] sts.

Dec 1 st at each end of next 5 rows, then on foll 3 alt rows, then on 4 [5: 6: 7: 8] foll 4th rows, then on foll 0 [0: 0: 1: 1] alt row. 67 [67: 67: 65: 65] sts.

Work 1 row, ending with RS facing for next row.

Break off yarn A and join in yarn B.

Beg with a K row, work in st st, dec 1 st at each end of next and foll 3 [3: 3: 2: 2] alt rows, then on foll 11 rows, ending with RS facing for next row. 37 sts.

Cast off 4 sts at beg of next 4 rows.

Cast off rem 21 sts.

MAKING UP

Press as described on the information page.

Join both shoulder seams using back stitch, or mattress stitch if preferred.

Neckband

Using 2¾ mm (US 2) needles and yarn A cast on 11 sts.

Work in g st until neckband, when slightly stretched, fits neatly around entire neck edge, beg and ending at front opening edges and ending with RS facing for next row.

Cast off.

Slip stitch neckband in place.

Button band

Using 2¾ mm (US 2) needles and yarn A cast on 11 sts.

Work in g st until this band, when slightly stretched, fits neatly up left front opening edge, from lower edge of hemband to top edge of neckband and ending with **WS** facing for next row.

Cast off knitwise (on **WS**).

Slip stitch button band in place.

Mark positions for 4 buttons on this band - first button to come 12 cm up from lower edge, top button to come 2 cm below upper edge, and rem 2 buttons evenly spaced between.

Buttonhole band

Work to match button band, with the addition of 4 buttonholes to correspond with positions marked for buttons as folls:

Buttonhole row (RS): K4, cast off 2 sts (to make a buttonhole - cast on 2 sts over these cast-off sts on next row), K to end.

See information page for finishing instructions, setting in sleeves using the set-in method.

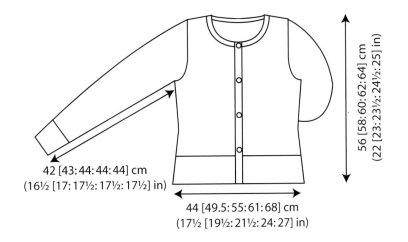

42 [43: 44: 44: 44] cm
(16½ [17: 17½: 17½: 17½] in)

56 [58: 60: 62: 64] cm
(22 [23: 23½: 24½: 25] in)

44 [49.5: 55: 61: 68] cm
(17½ [19½: 21½: 24: 27] in)

Main Image Page 24

Durian ✱
By Marie Wallin

SIZE

	S	M	L	XL	XXL	
To fit bust						
	81–86	91–97	102–107	112–117	122–127	cm
	32–34	36–38	40–42	44–46	48–50	in

YARN

Rowan Panama

7	7	8	9	11	x 50gm

(photographed in Nightshade 312)

NEEDLES

1 pair 2¾ mm (no 12) (US 2) needles
1 pair 3¼ mm (no 10) (US 3) needles

TENSION

27 sts and 36 rows to 10 cm measured over st st using 3¼ mm (US 3) needles.

BACK

Using 2¾ mm (US 2) needles cast on 135 [149: 165: 181: 199] sts.
Row 1 (RS): K1, *P1, K1, rep from * to end.
Row 2: As row 1.
These 2 rows form moss st.
Work in moss st for a further 4 rows, ending with RS facing for next row.
Change to 3¼ mm (US 3) needles.
Beg with a K row, work in st st until back meas 27 [28: 29: 30: 31] cm, ending with RS facing for next row.★★
Shape right cap sleeve
Inc 1 st at beg of next and foll 4th row, then on foll 5 alt rows, then inc 1 st at shaped edge on foll 4 rows, ending with **WS** facing for next row. 146 [160: 176: 192: 210] sts.
Place marker at beg of last row to denote base of right armhole opening.
Work 8 rows, ending with **WS** facing for next row.
Shape left armhole
Cast off 7 [9: 10: 11: 13] sts at beg of next row. 139 [151: 166: 181: 197] sts.
Dec 1 st at left armhole edge of next 7 [9: 11: 11: 13] rows, then on foll 8 [8: 9: 15: 18] alt rows, then on 2 [2: 2: 3: 2] foll 4th rows, then on

1 [2: 3: 1: 1] foll 6th rows. 121 [130: 141: 151: 163] sts.
Work 25 [21: 15: 13: 13] rows, ending with RS facing for next row.
Shape right shoulder
Cast off 11 [13: 15: 17: 19] sts at beg of next and foll alt row. 99 [104: 111: 117: 125] sts.
Work 1 row.
Shape back neck
Next row (RS): Cast off 12 [13: 15: 17: 19] sts, K until there are 16 [18: 19: 21: 23] sts on right needle and turn, leaving rem 71 [73: 77: 79: 83] sts on a holder.
Work each side of neck separately.
Cast off 4 sts at beg of next row.
Cast off rem 12 [14: 15: 17: 19] sts.
With RS facing, rejoin yarn to rem sts, cast off 57 [57: 59: 59: 61] sts, K to end. 14 [16: 18: 20: 22] sts.
Work 1 row.
Cast off 4 sts at beg of next row. 10 [12: 14: 16: 18] sts.
Work 1 row, ending with RS facing for next row.
Shape left shoulder
Cast off.

FRONT

Work as given for back to ★★.
Shape right cap sleeve
Inc 1 st at end of next and foll 4th row, then on foll 5 alt rows, then inc 1 st at shaped edge on foll 4 rows, ending with **WS** facing for next row. 146 [160: 176: 192: 210] sts.
Place marker at end of last row to denote base of right armhole opening.
Work 7 rows, ending with RS facing for next row.
Shape left armhole
Cast off 7 [9: 10: 11: 13] sts at beg of next row. 139 [151: 166: 181: 197] sts.
Work 1 row.
Dec 1 st at left armhole edge of next 7 [9: 11: 11: 13] rows, then on foll 8 [8: 9: 15: 18] alt rows, then on 2 [2: 2: 3: 2] foll 4th rows, then on 1 [2: 2: 0: 0] foll 6th rows. 121 [130: 142: 152: 164] sts.
Work 11 [7: 5: 3: 1] rows, ending with RS facing for next row.
Shape front neck
Next row (RS): (K2tog) 0 [0: 1: 0: 0] times, K20 [22: 24: 28: 31] and turn, leaving rem 101 [108: 116: 124: 133] sts on a holder.

Work each side of neck separately.

Dec 1 st at neck edge of next 8 rows, then on foll 2 [2: 2: 3: 3: 4] alt rows **and at same time** dec - [-: -: 1: 1] st at armhole edge of - [-: -: 2nd: 4th] row. 10 [12: 14: 16: 18] sts.

Work 7 rows, ending with RS facing for next row.

Shape left shoulder

Cast off.

With RS facing, rejoin yarn to rem sts, cast off 45 sts, K to end. 56 [63: 71: 79: 88] sts.

Dec 1 st at neck edge of next 8 rows, then on foll 2 [2: 2: 3: 3: 4] alt rows. 46 [53: 60: 68: 76] sts.

Work 2 rows, ending with **WS** facing for next row.

Shape right shoulder

Cast off 11 [13: 15: 17: 19] sts at beg of next and foll alt row, then 12 [13: 15: 17: 19] sts at beg of foll alt row.

Work 1 row.

Cast off rem 12 [14: 15: 17: 19] sts.

MAKING UP

Press as described on the information page.

Join right shoulder seam using back stitch, or mattress stitch if preferred.

Neckband

With RS facing and using 2¾ mm (US 2) needles, pick up and knit 16 [16: 18: 18: 20] sts down left side of neck, 45 sts from front, 16 [16: 18: 18: 20] sts up right side of neck, then 66 [66: 68: 68: 70] sts from back. 143 [143: 149: 149: 155] sts.

Work in moss st as given for back for 5 rows, ending with RS facing for next row.

Cast off in moss st.

Right cuff border

With RS facing and using 2¾ mm (US 2) needles, pick up and knit 107 [113: 119: 123: 129] sts evenly along right armhole opening edge between markers.

Work in moss st as given for back for 5 rows, ending with RS facing for next row.

Cast off in moss st.

Join left side seam.

Left armhole border

With RS facing and using 2¾ mm (US 2) needles, pick up and knit 121 [131: 137: 145: 155] sts evenly all round left armhole edge, beg and ending at shoulder edge.

Work in moss st as given for back for 5 rows, ending with RS facing for next row.

Cast off in moss st.

Join neckband seam.

Ties (both alike)

With RS facing and using 2¾ mm (US 2) needles, pick up and knit 18 [20: 22: 24: 26] sts evenly across left shoulder edge, between pick-up row of neckband and cast-off edge of armhole border.

Row 1 (WS): P2 [1: 2: 1: 2], (P2tog) 7 [9: 9: 11: 11] times, P2 [1: 2: 1: 2]. 11 [11: 13: 13: 15] sts.

Now work in moss st as given for back until tie meas 30 cm from pick-up row, ending with RS facing for next row.

Dec 1 st at each end of next and every foll alt row until 3 sts rem.

Work 1 row.

Next row (RS): Sl 1, work 2 tog, psso and fasten off.

Cast off in moss st.

See information page for finishing instructions.

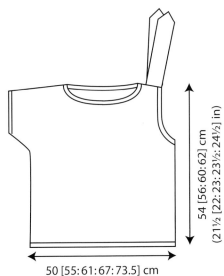

54 [56: 60: 62] cm
(21½ [22: 23: 23½: 24½] in)

50 [55: 61: 67: 73.5] cm
(19½ [21½: 24: 26½: 29] in)

Main Image Page 4

Guava ❋
By Marie Wallin

SIZE

	S	M	L	XL	XXL	
To fit bust						
	81–86	91–97	102–107	112–117	122–127	cm
	32–34	36–38	40–42	44–46	48–50	in

YARN
Rowan Panama

7	8	9	10	11	x 50gm

(photographed in Jacaranda 308)

NEEDLES
1 pair 2¾ mm (no 12) (US 2) needles
1 pair 3¼ mm (no 10) (US 3) needles
3¼ mm (no 10) (US 3) circular needle, 60 cm long

TENSION
27 sts and 36 rows to 10 cm measured over st st using 3¼ mm (US 3) needles.

BACK
Using 2¾ mm (US 2) needles cast on 123 [137: 153: 169: 189] sts.
Work in g st for 8 rows, ending with RS facing for next row.
Change to 3¼ mm (US 3) needles.
Beg with a K row, work in st st, dec 1 st at each end of next and 5 foll 4th rows, then on foll 3 alt rows. 105 [119: 135: 151: 171] sts.
Work 13 rows, ending with RS facing for next row.
Inc 1 st at each end of next and 3 foll 12th rows. 113 [127: 143: 159: 179] sts.
Cont straight until back meas 28 [29: 30: 31: 32] cm, ending with RS facing for next row.
Shape armholes
Cast off 4 [5: 6: 7: 8] sts at beg of next 2 rows. 105 [117: 131: 145: 163] sts.
Dec 1 st at each end of next 3 [5: 7: 9: 11] rows, then on foll 4 [5: 6: 7: 9] alt rows. 91 [97: 105: 113: 123] sts.
Cont straight until armhole meas 20 [21: 22: 23: 24] cm, ending with RS facing for next row.
Shape shoulders and back neck
Cast off 3 [4: 5: 7: 8] sts at beg of next 2 rows. 85 [89: 95: 99: 107] sts.
Next row (RS): Cast off 3 [4: 5: 7: 8] sts, K until there are 8 [9: 10: 10: 12] sts on right needle and turn, leaving rem sts on a holder.

Work each side of neck separately.
Cast off 4 sts at beg of next row.
Cast off rem 4 [5: 6: 6: 8] sts.
With RS facing, rejoin yarn to rem sts, cast off centre 63 [63: 65: 65: 67] sts, K to end.
Complete to match first side, reversing shapings.

FRONT
Work as given for back until 38 [38: 42: 42: 46] rows less have been worked than on back to beg of shoulder shaping, ending with RS facing for next row.
Shape front neck
Next row (RS): K25 [28: 32: 36: 41] and turn, leaving rem sts on a holder.
Work each side of neck separately.
Dec 1 st at neck edge of next 10 rows, then on foll 3 alt rows, then on 1 [1: 2: 2: 3] foll 4th rows, then on foll 6th row. 10 [13: 16: 20: 24] sts.
Work 11 rows, ending with RS facing for next row.
Shape shoulder
Cast off 3 [4: 5: 7: 8] sts at beg of next and foll alt row.
Work 1 row.
Cast off rem 4 [5: 6: 6: 8] sts.
With RS facing, rejoin yarn to rem sts, cast off centre 41 sts, K to end.
Complete to match first side, reversing shapings.

MAKING UP
Press as described on the information page.
Join both shoulder seams using back stitch, or mattress stitch if preferred.
Collar
With RS facing and using 3¼ mm (US 3) circular needle, pick up and knit 39 [39: 43: 43: 47] sts down left side of neck, 41 sts from front, 39 [39: 43: 43: 47] sts up right side of neck, then 71 [71: 73: 73: 75] sts from back. 190 [190: 200: 200: 210] sts.
Turn work so that **WS** of body is facing for next round - this is RS of collar.
Round 1 (RS of collar): Knit.
This round forms st st.
Work 18 rounds.
Round 20: (K5, M1, K5) 19 [19: 20: 20: 21] times. 209 [209: 220: 220: 231] sts.
Work 19 rounds.

Round 41: (K5, M1, K6) 19 [19: 20: 20: 21] times. 228 [228: 240: 240: 252] sts.

Work 19 rounds.

Round 61: (K6, M1, K6) 19 [19: 20: 20: 21] times. 247 [247: 260: 260: 273] sts.

Work 19 rounds.

Round 81: (K6, M1, K7) 19 [19: 20: 20: 21] times. 266 [266: 280: 280: 294] sts.

Work 19 rounds.

Round 101: Purl.

Round 102: Knit.

Cast off loosely **purlwise** (on RS).

Armhole borders (both alike)

With RS facing and using 3¼ mm (US 3) needles, pick up and knit 116 [124: 130: 138: 146] sts evenly all round armhole edge.

Work in g st for 8 rows, ending with **WS** facing for next row.

Cast off knitwise (on **WS**).

See information page for finishing instructions.

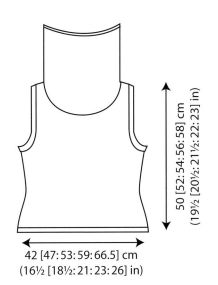

50 [52: 54: 56: 58] cm
(19½ [20½: 21½: 22: 23] in)

42 [47: 53: 59: 66.5] cm
(16½ [18½: 21: 23: 26] in)

Kaffir Dress ✺✺
By Lisa Richardson

Main Image Page 27

SIZE

	S	M	L	XL	XXL	
To fit bust						
	81–86	91–97	102–107	112–117	122–127	cm
	32–34	36–38	40–42	44–46	48–50	in

YARN

Rowan Panama

A	Cosmos 303					
	5	6	6	7	7	x 50gm
B	Morning Glory 302					
	2	2	2	2	2	x 50gm
C	Orchid 304					
	5	5	7	7	8	x 50gm
D	Hibiscus 311					
	2	2	2	2	4	x 50gm

NEEDLES

1 pair 2¾ mm (no 12) (US 2) needles
1 pair 3¼ mm (no 10) (US 3) needles

TENSION

27 sts and 38 rows to 10 cm measured over patt using 3¼ mm (US 3) needles.

STRIPE SEQUENCE

Rows 1 to 4: Using yarn A.
Rows 5 to 7: Using yarn B.
Rows 8 to 12: Using yarn C.
Rows 13 to 15: Using yarn D.
Rows 16 to 20: Using yarn A.
Rows 21 to 23: Using yarn C.
Rows 24 to 28: Using yarn B.

Rows 29 to 31: Using yarn C.
Rows 32 to 36: Using yarn D.
Rows 37 to 39: Using yarn B.
Rows 40 to 44: Using yarn C.
Rows 45 to 47: Using yarn A.
Rows 48 to 52: Using yarn B.
Rows 53 to 55: Using yarn C.
Rows 56 to 60: Using yarn D.
Rows 61 to 63: Using yarn A.
Rows 64 to 68: Using yarn C.
Rows 69 to 71: Using yarn B.
Rows 72 to 76: Using yarn C.
Rows 77 to 79: Using yarn D.
Rows 80 to 84: Using yarn B.
Rows 85 to 87: Using yarn C.
Rows 88 to 92: Using yarn A.
Rows 5 to 92 **only** form stripe sequence.

BACK (knitted sideways)
Right hip section
Using 3¼ mm (US 3) needles and yarn A cast on 70 [74: 74: 78: 82] sts.
Beg with stripe row 1, now work in stripe sequence (see above) and patt as folls:
Row 1 (RS): Knit.
Row 2: Purl.
Row 3: Cast on 10 sts, K to end.
Row 4: Knit.
Row 5: Cast on 8 sts, K to end.
Row 6: *P2tog, yrn, rep from * to last 2 sts, P2.
Row 7: Cast on 6 sts, K to end. 94 [98: 98: 102: 106] sts.
Row 8: Knit.
These 8 rows form patt and beg side seam shaping.
Keeping patt and stripe sequence correct, cast on 4 sts at beg of next row, then 3 sts at beg of foll 4 alt rows, then 4 sts at beg of foll alt row, and 5 sts at beg of foll alt row, taking inc sts into patt. 119 [123: 123: 127: 131] sts.
Work 1 row, ending after patt row 6 and stripe row 22 and with RS facing for next row.
Break yarn and leave sts on a holder.
Right shoulder section
Using 3¼ mm (US 3) needles and yarn A cast on 30 [32: 36: 38: 40] sts.
Beg with stripe row **17**, now work in stripe sequence (see above) and patt as folls:
Row 1 (RS): Knit.
Row 2: Cast on 8 sts, P to end.
Row 3: (Inc in first st) 1 [1: 1: 1: 0] times, K to end.
Row 4: Cast on 8 sts, K to end.
Row 5: Inc in first st, K to end.
Row 6: Cast on 8 sts, now work across these 8 sts and rest of row as folls: P1, *P2tog, yrn, rep from * to last 1 [1: 1: 1: 2] sts, P1 [1: 1: 1: 2]. 56 [58: 62: 64: 65] sts.
Join sections
Next row (RS): Work across shoulder section sts as folls: (inc in first st) 1 [1: 1: 1: 0] times, K to end, turn and cast on 40 sts, turn and K across 119 [123: 123: 127: 131] sts of hip section. 216 [222: 226: 232: 236] sts.
**Now beg with patt row 8 and stripe row 24, cont in patt and stripe

sequence across all sts and shape shoulder seam as folls:
Inc 1 st at beg of 2nd and foll 17 [12: 8: 2: 0] alt rows, then on 1 [6: 10: 16: 20] foll 4th rows, taking inc sts into patt. 235 [241: 245: 251: 257] sts.
Work 3 rows, ending with RS facing for next row.
Place marker at end of last row to denote right shoulder point.**
Shape back neck
Keeping patt correct, dec 1 st at marked edge of next 3 rows, then on foll 2 alt rows, then on 3 foll 4th rows. 227 [233: 237: 243: 249] sts.
Work 27 [27: 31: 31: 35] rows, ending with RS facing for next row.
Inc 1 st at marked edge of next and 3 foll 4th rows, then on foll 2 alt rows, then on foll 2 rows, taking inc sts into patt. 235 [241: 245: 251: 257] sts.
Place marker at beg of last row to denote left shoulder point.
***Work 3 rows, ending with RS facing for next row.
Now shape left shoulder seam as folls:
Dec 1 st at beg of next and 1 [6: 10: 16: 20] foll 4th rows, then on foll 17 [12: 8: 2: 0] alt rows. 216 [222: 226: 232: 236] sts.
Work 1 row, ending with RS facing for next row.
Shape left shoulder section
Next row (RS): (Work 2 tog) 1 [1: 1: 1: 0] times, patt 55 [57: 61: 63: 65] sts and turn, leaving rem 159 [163: 163: 167: 171] sts on a holder.
Work on this set of sts only for left shoulder section.
Keeping patt correct, cast off 8 sts at beg of next and foll 2 alt rows **and at same time** dec 1 st at shoulder edge of 2nd and foll 1 [1: 1: 1: 0] alt row, ending with RS facing for next row.
Cast off rem 30 [32: 36: 38: 40] sts.
Shape left hip section
With RS facing, rejoin appropriate yarn to rem sts, cast off next 40 sts, patt to end. 119 [123: 123: 127: 131] sts.
Work 1 row, ending with RS facing for next row.
Keeping patt correct, cast off 5 sts at beg of next row, 4 sts at beg of foll alt row, 3 sts at beg of foll 4 alt rows, 4 sts at beg of foll alt row, 6 sts at beg of foll alt row, 8 sts at beg of foll alt row, then 10 sts at beg of foll alt row.
Work 1 row, ending with RS facing for next row.
Cast off rem 70 [74: 74: 78: 82] sts.

FRONT
Right hip section
Using 3¼ mm (US 3) needles and yarn A cast on 70 [74: 74: 78: 82] sts.
Beg with stripe row 1, now work in stripe sequence (see above) and patt as folls:
Row 1 (WS): Purl.
Row 2: Knit.
Row 3: Cast on 10 sts, P to end.
Row 4: Purl.
Row 5: Cast on 8 sts, P to end.
Row 6: *K2tog, yfwd, rep from * to last 2 sts, K2.
Row 7: Cast on 6 sts, P to end. 94 [98: 98: 102: 106] sts.
Row 8: Purl.
These 8 rows form patt and beg side seam shaping.
Keeping patt and stripe sequence correct, cast on 4 sts at beg of next row, then 3 sts at beg of foll 4 alt rows, then 4 sts at beg of foll alt row, and 5 sts at beg of foll alt row, taking inc sts into patt. 119 [123: 123: 127: 131] sts.
Work 1 row, ending after patt row 6 and stripe row 22 and with **WS

facing for next row.

Break yarn and leave sts on a holder.

Right shoulder section

Using 3¼ mm (US 3) needles and yarn A cast on 30 [32: 36: 38: 40] sts.

Beg with stripe row **17**, now work in stripe sequence (see above) and patt as folls:

Row 1 (WS): Purl.

Row 2: Cast on 8 sts, K to end.

Row 3: (Inc in first st) 1 [1: 1: 1: 0] times, P to end.

Row 4: Cast on 8 sts, P to end.

Row 5: Inc in first st, P to end.

Row 6: Cast on 8 sts, now work across these 8 sts and rest of row as folls: K1, ★K2tog, yfwd, rep from ★ to last 1 [1: 1: 1: 2] sts, K1 [1: 1: 1: 2]. 56 [58: 62: 64: 65] sts.

Join sections

Next row (WS): Work across shoulder section sts as folls: (inc in first st) 1 [1: 1: 1: 0] times, P to end, turn and cast on 40 sts, turn and P across 119 [123: 123: 127: 131] sts of hip section. 216 [222: 226: 232: 236] sts.

Reading RS for WS and vice versa, now work as given for back from ★★ to ★★.

Shape front neck

Keeping patt correct, dec 1 st at marked edge of next 7 rows, then on foll 4 alt rows, then on 3 foll 4th rows, then on 2 foll 6th rows. 219 [225: 229: 235: 241] sts.

Work 75 [75: 79: 79: 83] rows, ending with RS facing for next row.

Inc 1 st at marked edge of next and 2 foll 6th rows, then on 3 foll 4th rows, then on foll 4 alt rows, then on foll 6 rows, taking inc sts into patt. 235 [241: 245: 251: 257] sts.

Place marker at beg of last row to denote left shoulder point.

Complete as given for back from ★★★, still reading RS for WS and vice versa.

MAKING UP

Press as described on the information page.

Join right shoulder seam using back stitch, or mattress stitch if preferred.

Back hem border

With RS facing, using 2¾ mm (US 2) needles and yarn C, pick up and knit 140 [154: 168: 184: 204] sts evenly along straight (lower) row-end edge of back.

Work in g st for 4 rows, ending with **WS** facing for next row.

Cast off knitwise (on **WS**).

Front hem border

With RS facing, using 2¾ mm (US 2) needles and yarn C, pick up and knit 202 [216: 230: 246: 266] sts evenly along straight (lower) row-end edge of front.

Work in g st for 4 rows, ending with **WS** facing for next row.

Cast off knitwise (on **WS**).

Neckband

With RS facing, using 2¾ mm (US 2) needles and yarn C, pick up and knit 27 sts down left side of front neck, 53 [53: 56: 56: 59] sts from front, 27 sts up right side of front neck, then 46 [46: 49: 49: 52] sts from back. 153 [153: 159: 159: 165] sts.

Work in g st for 4 rows, ending with **WS** facing for next row.

Cast off knitwise (on **WS**).

Armhole borders (both alike)

With RS facing, using 2¾ mm (US 2) needles and yarn C, pick up and knit 60 [64: 72: 76: 80] sts along armhole cast-on (or cast-off) edge.

Work in g st for 4 rows, ending with **WS** facing for next row.

Cast off knitwise (on **WS**).

See information page for finishing instructions.

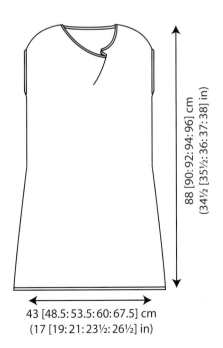

88 [90: 92: 94: 96] cm
(34½ [35½: 36: 37: 38] in)

43 [48.5: 53.5: 60: 67.5] cm
(17 [19: 21: 23½: 26½] in)

Mango ✱✱

By Lisa Richardson

Main Image Page 20

SIZE

	S	M	L	XL	XXL	
To fit bust						
	81–86	91–97	102–107	112–117	122–127	cm
	32–34	36–38	40–42	44–46	48–50	in

YARN

Rowan Panama

13	15	17	18	20	x 50gm

(photographed in Tulip 307)

NEEDLES

1 pair 2¾ mm (no 12) (US 2) needles
1 pair 3¼ mm (no 10) (US 3) needles

TENSION

30 sts and 40 rows to 10 cm measured over bodice patt using 3¼ mm (US 3) needles.

SPECIAL ABBREVIATIONS

Cr3 = K into front of 3rd st on left needle, then into front of 2nd st on left needle, then into front of first st and slip all 3 sts off left needle together.

BACK

Using 3¼ mm (US 3) needles cast on 174 [188: 216: 244: 272] sts.
Row 1 (RS): K1, ★K2tog, (yfwd) twice, sl 1, K1, psso, K3, rep from ★ to last 5 sts, K2tog, (yfwd) twice, sl 1, K1, psso, K1.
Row 2: K2, ★(K1 tbl, K1) into double yfwd of previous row, K1, P3, K1, rep from ★ to last 4 sts, (K1 tbl, K1) into double yfwd of previous row, K2.
Row 3: K1, ★K2tog, (yfwd) twice, sl 1, K1, psso, Cr3, rep from ★ to last 5 sts, K2tog, (yfwd) twice, sl 1, K1, psso, K1.
Row 4: As row 2.
These 4 rows form lace patt.
Cont in lace patt until back meas 34 [35: 36: 37: 38] cm, ending after patt row 4 and with RS facing for next row.
Next row (RS): K1, ★K2tog, yfwd, sl 1, K1, psso, K3, rep from ★ to last 5 sts, K2tog, yfwd, sl 1, K1, psso, K1. 149 [161: 185: 209: 233] sts.
Next row: K2, ★K2, P3, K1, rep from ★ to last 3 sts, K3.

Next row: K1, ★K1, sl 1, K1, psso, Cr3, rep from ★ to last 4 sts, K1, sl 1, K1, psso, K1. 124 [134: 154: 174: 194] sts.
Next row: K2tog, ★K1, P3, K1, rep from ★ to last 2 sts, K2tog. 122 [132: 152: 172: 192] sts.
Now work in bodice patt as folls:
Row 1 (RS): Knit.
Row 2: K2, ★P3, K2, rep from ★ to end.
Row 3: K2, ★Cr3, K2, rep from ★ to end.
Row 4: As row 2.
These 4 rows form bodice patt.
Cont in bodice patt, inc 1 st at each end of 5th and 4 foll 10th rows, taking inc sts into patt. 132 [142: 162: 182: 202] sts.
Cont straight until back meas 50 [51: 52: 53: 54] cm, ending with RS facing for next row.
Shape armholes
Keeping patt correct, cast off 5 [7: 9: 11: 13] sts at beg of next 2 rows. 122 [128: 144: 160: 176] sts.
Dec 1 st at each end of next 5 [7: 9: 11: 13] rows, then on foll 5 [3: 4: 6: 7] alt rows. 102 [108: 118: 126: 136] sts.
Cont straight until armhole meas 19 [20: 21: 22: 23] cm, ending with RS facing for next row.
Shape back neck
Next row (RS): Patt 28 [31: 34: 38: 42] sts and turn, leaving rem sts on a holder.
Work each side of neck separately.
Keeping patt correct, dec 1 st at neck edge of next 3 rows, ending with RS facing for next row. 25 [28: 31: 35: 39] sts.
Shape shoulder
Cast off 5 [6: 7: 8: 9] sts at beg of next and foll 2 alt rows **and at same time** dec 1 st at neck edge of next 3 rows, then foll alt row.
Work 1 row.
Cast off rem 6 [6: 6: 7: 8] sts.
With RS facing, rejoin yarn to rem sts, cast off centre 46 [46: 50: 50: 52] sts, patt to end.
Complete to match first side, reversing shapings.

FRONT

Work as given for back until 20 [20: 24: 24: 28] rows less have been worked than on back to beg of **shoulder** shaping, ending with RS facing for next row.

Shape neck

Next row (RS): Patt 33 [36: 40: 44: 49] sts and turn, leaving rem sts on a holder.

Work each side of neck separately.

Keeping patt correct, dec 1 st at neck edge of next 8 rows, then on foll 3 alt rows, then on 1 [1: 2: 2: 3] foll 4th rows. 21 [24: 27: 31: 35] sts.

Work 1 row, ending with RS facing for next row.

Shape shoulder

Cast off 5 [6: 7: 8: 9] sts at beg of next and foll 2 alt rows.

Work 1 row.

Cast off rem 6 [6: 6: 7: 8] sts.

With RS facing, rejoin yarn to rem sts, cast off centre 36 [36: 38: 38: 38] sts, patt to end.

Complete to match first side, reversing shapings.

SLEEVES

Using 3¼ mm (US 3) needles cast on 97 [97: 104: 104: 111] sts.

Work in lace patt as given for back until sleeve meas 11 cm, ending after patt row 4 and with RS facing for next row.

Next row (RS): K1, *K2tog, yfwd, sl 1, K1, psso, K3, rep from * to last 5 sts, K2tog, yfwd, sl 1, K1, psso, K1. 83 [83: 89: 89: 95] sts.

Next row: K2, *K2, P3, K1, rep from * to last 3 sts, K3.

Next row: K1, *K1, sl 1, K1, psso, Cr3, rep from * to last 4 sts, K1, sl 1, K1, psso, K1. 69 [69: 74: 74: 79] sts.

Next row: K2tog, *K1, P3, K1, rep from * to last 2 sts, K2tog. 67 [67: 72: 72: 77] sts.

Now work in bodice patt as given for back, shaping sides by inc 1 st at each end of 5th [5th: 5th: 3rd: 3rd] and every foll 6th row to 71 [91: 92:

114: 119] sts, then on every foll 8th row until there are 97 [103: 108: –: –] sts, taking inc sts into patt.

Cont straight until sleeve meas 46 [47: 48: 48: 48] cm, ending with RS facing for next row.

Shape top

Keeping patt correct, cast off 5 [7: 9: 11: 13] sts at beg of next 2 rows. 87 [89: 90: 92: 93] sts.

Dec 1 st at each end of next 5 rows, then on foll 4 alt rows, then on 4 foll 4th rows. 61 [63: 64: 66: 67] sts.

Work 1 row.

Dec 1 st at each end of next and every foll alt row to 47 [47: 48: 48: 49] sts, then on foll 7 rows, ending with RS facing for next row. 33 [33: 34: 34: 35] sts.

Cast off 4 sts at beg of next 4 rows.

Cast off rem 17 [17: 18: 18: 19] sts.

MAKING UP

Press as described on the information page.

Join right shoulder seam using back stitch, or mattress stitch if preferred.

Neckband

With RS facing and using 2¾ mm (US 2) needles, pick up and knit 20 [20: 24: 24: 28] sts down left side of neck, 32 [32: 34: 34: 34] sts from front, 20 [20: 24: 24: 28] sts up right side of neck, then 60 [60: 64: 64: 66] sts from back. 132 [132: 146: 146: 156] sts.

Work in g st for 8 rows, ending with **WS** facing for next row.

Cast off knitwise (on **WS**).

See information page for finishing instructions, setting in sleeves using the set-in method.

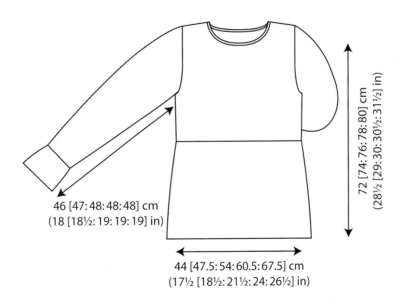

46 [47: 48: 48: 48] cm
(18 [18½: 19: 19: 19] in)

72 [74: 76: 78: 80] cm
(28½ [29: 30: 30½: 31½] in)

44 [47.5: 54: 60.5: 67.5] cm
(17½ [18½: 21½: 24: 26½] in)

Main Image Page 8

Mangosteen ✳
By Grace Melville

SIZE

	S	M	L	XL	XXL	
To fit bust						
	81-86	91-97	102-107	112-117	122-127	cm
	32-34	36-38	40-42	44-46	48-50	in

YARN

Rowan Panama

10	10	12	13	15	x 50gm

(photographed in Lotus 309)

NEEDLES

1 pair 2¾ mm (no 12) (US 2) needles
1 pair 3¼ mm (no 10) (US 3) needles

BUTTONS - 1x RW5021 (15mm) from Bedecked. See information page for contact details.

TENSION

27 sts and 36 rows to 10 cm measured over st st using 3¼ mm (US 3) needles.

BACK

Using 3¼ mm (US 3) needles cast on 175 [189: 205: 221: 239] sts.
Beg with a K row, work in st st until back meas 34 [35: 36: 37: 38] cm, ending with RS facing for next row.
Next row (RS): K1, (K4tog) 4 times, (sl 1, K2tog, psso) 12 times, K to last 53 sts, (sl 1, K2tog, psso) 12 times, (K4tog) 4 times, K1. 103 [117: 133: 149: 167] sts.
Next row (WS): K17, P to last 17 sts, K17.
Next row: Knit.
Rep last 2 rows 4 times more, then first of these rows again, ending with RS facing for next row.
Next row (RS): (K2, M1) 8 times, K to last 16 sts, (M1, K2) 8 times. 119 [133: 149: 165: 183] sts.
Beg with a P row, work in st st until back meas 51 [52: 53: 54: 55] cm, ending with RS facing for next row.
Place markers at both ends of last row to denote base of armhole openings.
Next row (RS): Knit.

Next row: K1, P to last st, K1.
Last 2 rows set the sts - first and last st of every row worked as a K st with all other sts still in st st.★★
Work 1 row, ending with **WS** facing for next row.
Next row (WS): K1, P58 [65: 73: 81: 90], inc knitwise in next st, P to last st, K1. 120 [134: 150: 166: 184] sts.
Divide for back opening
Next row (RS): K60 [67: 75: 83: 92] and turn, leaving rem sts on a holder.
Work each side of neck separately.
Next row (WS): K1, P to last st, K1.
Next row: Knit.
Last 2 rows set the sts - first and last st of every row worked as a K st with all other sts still in st st.
Cont straight until work meas 23 [24: 25: 26: 27] cm from markers, ending with **WS** facing for next row.
Shape back neck
Cast off 28 [28: 29: 29: 30] sts at beg of next row, then 5 sts at beg of foll alt row. 27 [34: 41: 49: 57] sts.
Dec 1 st at neck edge of next 3 rows. 24 [31: 38: 46: 54] sts.
Work 1 row, ending with RS facing for next row.
Shape shoulder
Cast off.
With RS facing, rejoin yarn to rem sts, K to end.
Next row (WS): K1, P to last st, K1.
Next row: Knit.
Last 2 rows set the sts - first and last st of every row worked as a K st with all other sts still in st st.
Complete to match first side, reversing shapings.

FRONT
Work as given for back to ★★.
Cont straight until 22 [22: 24: 24: 26] rows less have been worked than on back to shoulder cast-off, ending with RS facing for next row.
Shape front neck
Next row (RS): K36 [43: 51: 59: 68] and turn, leaving rem sts on a holder.
Work each side of neck separately.
Dec 1 st at neck edge of next 8 rows, then on foll 3 [3: 4: 4: 5] alt rows, then on foll 4th row. 24 [31: 38: 46: 54] sts.

Work 3 rows, ending with RS facing for next row.
Shape shoulder
Cast off.
With RS facing, rejoin yarn to rem sts, cast off centre 47 sts, K to end.
Complete to match first side, reversing shapings.

MAKING UP
Press as described on the information page.
Join right shoulder seam using back stitch, or mattress stitch if preferred.
Neckband
With RS facing and using 2¾ mm (US 2) needles, beg and ending at back opening edges, pick up and knit 36 [36: 37: 37: 38] sts up left side of back neck, 22 [22: 24: 24: 26] sts down left side of front neck, 47 sts from front, 22 [22: 24: 24: 26] sts up right side of front neck, then 36 [36: 37: 37: 38] sts down right side of back neck. 163 [163: 169: 169: 175] sts.
Row 1 (WS): Knit.
Row 2: K1, (yfwd, lift st on right needle over the "yfwd" and off right needle) 6 times (to make button loop), K to end.
Cast off knitwise (on **WS**).
See information page for finishing instructions. Using photograph as a guide, at shoulder point, fold armhole edge back onto shoulder to form 4 cm turn-back and secure in place.

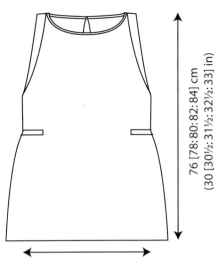

Main Image Page 30

Papaya ❋❋
By Grace Melville

SIZE

	S	M	L	XL	XXL	
To fit bust						
	81–86	91–97	102–107	112–117	122–127	cm
	32–34	36–38	40–42	44–46	48–50	in

YARN
Rowan Panama

5	6	6	7	8		x 50gm

(photographed in Dahlia 305)

NEEDLES
1 pair 3¾ mm (no 10) (US 3) needles
1 pair 4½ mm (no 7) (US 7) needles

TENSION
21 sts and 27 rows to 10 cm measured over st st using 4½ mm (US 7) needles.

BACK
Using 4½ mm (US 7) needles cast on 97 [107: 119: 133: 147] sts.
Beg with a K row, work in st st as folls:
Dec 1 st at each end of 21st and foll 20th row. 93 [103: 115: 129: 143] sts.
Cont straight until back meas 23 [24: 25: 26: 27] cm, ending with RS facing for next row.
Shape armholes
Cast off 3 [4: 5: 6: 7] sts at beg of next 2 rows. 87 [95: 105: 117: 129] sts.
Dec 1 st at each end of next 3 [5: 5: 7: 9] rows, then on foll 3 [3: 4: 5: 6] alt rows. 75 [79: 87: 93: 99] sts.

Work 3 [5: 5: 3: 3] rows, ending with RS facing for next row.

Now work in yoke patt as folls:

Rows 1 and 2: Knit.

Row 3 (RS): K to end, wrapping yarn twice round needle for every st.

Row 4: K to end, dropping extra loops.

Row 5: Knit.

Row 6: Purl.

Rows 7 to 10: As rows 5 and 6, twice.

These 10 rows form yoke patt.

Cont in yoke patt until armhole meas approx 21 [22: 23: 24: 25] cm, ending after patt row 4 and with RS facing for next row.

Shape shoulders and back neck

Cast off 4 [5: 6: 7: 7] sts at beg of next 2 rows. 67 [69: 75: 79: 85] sts.

Next row (RS): Cast off 4 [5: 6: 7: 7] sts, K until there are 8 [8: 9: 10: 12] sts on right needle and turn, leaving rem sts on a holder.

Work each side of neck separately.

Cast off 4 sts at beg of next row.

Cast off rem 4 [4: 5: 6: 8] sts.

With RS facing, rejoin yarn to rem sts, cast off centre 43 [43: 45: 45: 47] sts, K to end.

Complete to match first side, reversing shapings.

FRONT

Lower right front

Using 4½ mm (US 7) needles cast on 21 [22: 23: 24: 25] sts.

Beg with a K row, work in st st as folls:

Work 6 rows, ending with RS facing for next row.

Row 7 (RS): K to last 2 sts, inc in next st, K1.

Working all increases as set by last row, inc 1 st at end of 4th and 11 [11: 9: 5: 3] foll 4th rows, then on foll 24 [23: 26: 33: 36] alt rows, ending with **WS** facing for next row. 58 [58: 60: 64: 66] sts.

Next row (WS): Inc purlwise in first st, P to end.

Working all increases as now set, inc 1 st at shaped edge of next 4 [10: 16: 22: 28] rows, ending with RS facing for next row.

Break yarn and leave 63 [69: 77: 87: 95] sts on a holder.

Lower left front

Using 4½ mm (US 7) needles cast on 21 [22: 23: 24: 25] sts.

Beg with a K row, work in st st as folls:

Work 20 rows, ending with RS facing for next row.

Row 21 (RS): Inc in first st, K to end.

Working all increases as set by last row, inc 1 st at beg of 20th and 2 foll 16th rows, then on 2 [2: 1: 1: 1] foll 8th rows, then on 2 [1: 2: 2: 1] foll 6th rows, then on 1 [3: 4: 4: 4] foll 4th rows, then on 1 [1: 1: 2: 6] foll alt rows, ending with **WS** facing for next row. 31 [33: 35: 37: 41] sts.

Next row (WS): P to last 2 sts, inc purlwise in next st, P1.

Working all increases as now set, inc 1 st at shaped edge of next 0 [2: 4: 6: 8] rows, ending with RS facing for next row. 32 [36: 40: 44: 50] sts.

Join lower fronts

Next row (RS): Work across sts of lower left front as folls: cast on 2 sts, K to end, now work across sts of lower right front as folls: K to end. 97 [107: 110: 133: 147] sts.

Beg with a P row, work in st st as folls:

Dec 1 st at each end of 20th and foll 20th row. 93 [103: 115: 129: 143] sts.

Cont straight until front meas 23 [24: 25: 26: 27] cm **from joining row**, ending with RS facing for next row.

Now work as given for back from beg of armhole shaping until 14 [14: 16: 16: 18] rows less have been worked than on back to beg of shoulder shaping, ending with RS facing for next row.

Shape front neck

Next row (RS): K22 [24: 28: 31: 34] and turn, leaving rem sts on a holder.

Work each side of neck separately.

Keeping patt correct, dec 1 st at neck edge of next 7 rows, then on foll 3 [3: 4: 4: 5] alt rows. 12 [14: 17: 20: 22] sts.

Work 1 row, ending after patt row 4 and with RS facing for next row.

Shape shoulder

Cast off 4 [5: 6: 7: 7] sts at beg of next and foll alt row.

Work 1 row.

Cast off rem 4 [4: 5: 6: 8] sts.

With RS facing, rejoin yarn to rem sts, cast off centre 31 sts, K to end.

Complete to match first side, reversing shapings.

SLEEVES

Using 3¼ mm (US 3) needles cast on 67 [71: 75: 79: 83] sts.

Work in g st for 6 rows, ending with RS facing for next row.

Change to 4½ mm (US 7) needles.

Beg with a K row, work in st st until sleeve meas 3 cm, ending with RS facing for next row.

Shape top

Cast off 3 [4: 5: 6: 7] sts at beg of next 2 rows. 61 [63: 65: 67: 69] sts.

Dec 1 st at each end of next 5 rows, then on foll 3 [1: 1: 1: 1] alt rows, then on 0 [1: 1: 1: 2] foll 4th rows, then on foll 0 [2: 3: 4: 4] alt rows. 45 sts.

Work 1 row, ending with RS facing for next row.

Beg with row 1, now work in yoke patt as given for back, dec 1 st at each end of next and foll 4 alt rows, then on foll 7 rows, ending after patt row 6 and with RS facing for next row.

Cast off rem 21 sts.

MAKING UP

Press as described on the information page.

Join right shoulder seam using back stitch, or mattress stitch if preferred.

Neckband

With RS facing and using 3¼ mm (US 3) needles, pick up and knit 14 [14: 16: 16: 18] sts down left side of neck, 39 sts from front, 14 [14: 16: 16: 18] sts up right side of neck, then 65 [65: 67: 67: 69] sts from back. 132 [132: 138: 138: 144] sts.

Work in g st for 6 rows, ending with **WS** facing for next row.

Cast off knitwise (on **WS**).

See information page for finishing instructions, setting in sleeves using the set-in method.

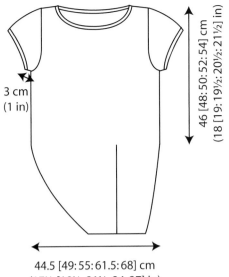

46 [48: 50: 52: 54] cm
(18 [19: 19½: 20½: 21½] in)

3 cm
(1 in)

44.5 [49: 55: 61.5: 68] cm
(17½ [19½: 21½: 24: 27] in)

Passion ❋❋

By Marie Wallin

Main Image Page 7

SIZE

	S	M	L	XL	XXL	
To fit bust						
	81–86	91–97	102–107	112–117	122–127	cm
	32–34	36–38	40–42	44–46	48–50	in

YARN

Rowan Panama

8	9	10	11	12	x 50gm

(photographed in Hibiscus 311)

NEEDLES

1 pair 3¼ mm (no 10) (US 3) needles

2¾ mm (no 12) (US 2) circular needles, 60 cm long

2.50mm (no 12) (US C2) crochet hook – optional

TENSION

27 sts and 36 rows to 10 cm measured over patt using 3¼ mm (US 3) needles.

CROCHET ABBREVIATIONS

ch = chain; **dc** = double crochet.

BACK and FRONT (both alike)

Using 3¼ mm (US 3) needles cast on 141 [153: 171: 187: 205] sts.

Row 1 (WS): Purl.

Following appropriate chart for size and section being knitted, working first 6 [7: 6: 9: 8] sts and last 5 [6: 5: 8: 7] sts as shown on chart, repeating the 10 st patt rep 13 [14: 16: 17: 19] times across each row and repeating the 28 row patt rep throughout, now work in patt from chart as folls: Work straight until work meas 28 [29: 30: 31: 32] cm, ending with RS facing for next row.

Shape raglan armholes

Keeping patt correct, cast off 3 sts at beg of next 2 rows. 135 [147: 165: 181: 199] sts.

Dec 1 st at each end of next 21 [29: 41: 46: 50] rows, then on foll 6 [4: 0: 0: 0] alt rows. 81 [81: 83: 89: 99] sts.

Work 1 [1: 1: 0: 0] row, ending with RS facing for next row.

Cast off.

SLEEVES

Using 3¼ mm (US 3) needles cast on 81 [85: 89: 93: 97] sts.

Row 1 (WS): Purl.

Following appropriate chart for size and section being knitted, working first 6 [8: 10: 7: 9] sts and last 5 [7: 9: 6: 8] sts as shown on chart, repeating the 10 st patt rep 7 [7: 7: 8: 8] times across each row and repeating the 28 row patt rep throughout, now work in patt from chart as folls:

Cont straight until sleeve meas 11 cm, ending with RS facing for next row.

Inc 1 st at each end of next and every foll alt row to 101 [103: 103: 107: 111] sts, then on every foll 4th row until there are 113 [117: 121: 125: 129] sts, taking inc sts into st st until there are sufficient to work in patt.

Work straight until sleeve meas 27 [28: 29: 29: 29] cm, ending with RS facing for next row.

Shape raglan armholes

Keeping patt correct, cast off 3 sts at beg of next 2 rows. 107 [111: 115: 119: 123] sts.

Dec 1 st at each end of next 17 rows, then on every foll alt row until 57 sts rem.

Work 1 row, ending with RS facing for next row.

Cast off.

MAKING UP

Press as described on the information page.

Join all raglan seams using back stitch, or mattress stitch if preferred.

Neckband

With RS facing and using 2¾ mm (US 2) circular needle, pick up and knit 57 sts from top of left sleeve, 81 [81: 81: 87: 99] sts from front, 57 sts from top of right sleeve, then 81 [81: 81: 87: 99] sts from back. 276 [276: 276: 288: 312] sts.

Round 1 (RS): ★K1, P1, yon, K2tog tbl, P1, K1, rep from ★ to end.

Round 2: K1, ★P1, K2, rep from ★ to last 2 sts, P1, K1.

Round 3: ★K1, P1, K2tog, yfrn, P1, K1, rep from ★ to end.

Round 4: As round 2.

These 4 rounds form patt.

Work in patt for a further 11 rounds.

Cast off in patt.

See information page for finishing instructions.

Waist tie

Using 2.50mm (US C2) crochet hook, make a ch approx 140 [150: 160: 170: 180] cm long, 1 dc into 2nd ch from hook, 1 dc into each ch to end.

Fasten off.

(Alternatively, make a twisted cord required length.)

Thread waist tie through eyelet holes of patt approx 16 [16: 16: 17: 17] cm up from cast-on edge and tie ends in a bow at centre front.

Sleeve ties (make 2)

Using 2.50mm (US C2) crochet hook, make a ch approx 50 [55: 55: 60: 60] cm long, 1 dc into 2nd ch from hook, 1 dc into each ch to end.

Fasten off.

(Alternatively, make 2 twisted cords required length.)

Thread sleeve tie through eyelet holes of patt approx 11 cm up from cast-on edge and tie ends in a bow on top of sleeve.

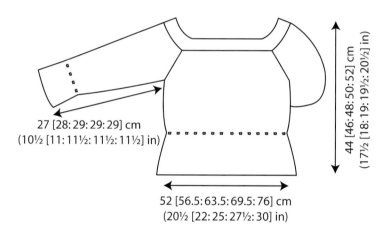

27 [28: 29: 29: 29] cm
(10½ [11: 11½: 11½: 11½] in)

44 [46: 48: 50: 52] cm
(17½ [18: 19: 19½: 20½] in)

52 [56.5: 63.5: 69.5: 76] cm
(20½ [22: 25: 27½: 30] in)

body size S/L & sleeve size S

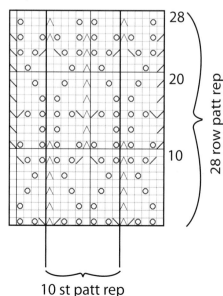

28

20

10

28 row patt rep

10 st patt rep

body size M & sleeves size XXL

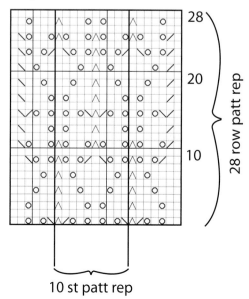

28

20

10

28 row patt rep

10 st patt rep

key

☐ K on RS, P on WS

▨ K2tog

◪ sl 1, K1, psso

◩ sl 1, K2tog, psso

▣ yfwd

sleeve size L

28

20

10

28 row patt rep

10 st patt rep

body size XL, sleeves size XXL

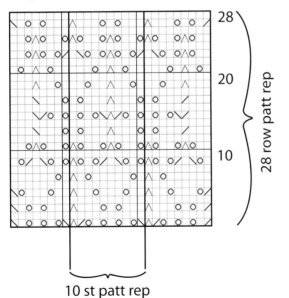

28

20

10

28 row patt rep

10 st patt rep

body size XXl & sleeves size M

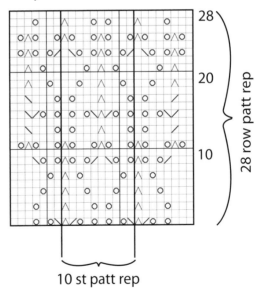

28

20

10

28 row patt rep

10 st patt rep

Peach ❉❉
By Marie Wallin

Main Image Page 14

SIZE

	S	M	L	XL	XXL	
To fit bust						
	81-86	91-97	102-107	112-117	122-127	cm
	32-34	36-38	40-42	44-46	48-50	in

YARN
Rowan Panama

A Aster 310						
	3	3	3	3	1	x 50gm
B Jacaranda 308						
	2	2	2	2	2	x 50gm
C Morning Glory 302						
	1	1	1	1	1	x 50gm
D Cosmos 303						
	2	2	2	2	3	x 50gm
E Lotus 309						
	5	6	6	7	7	x 50gm

NEEDLES
1 pair 2¾mm (no 12) (US 2) needles
1 pair 3¼ mm (no 10) (US 3) needles
2¾mm (no 12) (US 2) circular needle, 40 cm long
3¼ mm (no 10) (US 3) circular needle, 100 cm long

TENSION
27 sts and 36 rows to 10 cm measured over st st using 3¼ mm (US 3) needles.

STRIPE SEQUENCE
Rows 1 and 2: Using yarn B.
Rows 3 and 4: Using yarn C.
Rows 5 to 8: Using yarn C.
Rows 9 to 14: Using yarn E.
Rows 15 to 22: Using yarn A.
Rows 23 and 24: Using yarn B.
These 24 rows form stripe sequence and are repeated. (**Note**: First 2 and last 2 rows are worked in same colour, creating a 4 row stripe.)

BACK
Using 2¾mm (US 2) needles and yarn A cast on 200 [214: 230: 246: 264] sts.
Work in g st for 18 rows, ending with RS facing for next row.
Change to 3¼ mm (US 3) needles.
Beg with a K row and stripe row 1, now work in st st in stripe sequence (see above) throughout as folls:
Work 2 rows, ending with RS facing for next row.
★★Cast on 4 [4: 4: 3: 3] sts at beg of next 6 [10: 24: 8: 24] rows, then 5 [5: 5: 4: 4] sts at beg of foll 20 [18: 8: 28: 16] rows. 324 [344: 366: 382: 400] sts. (**Note**: As there becomes too many sts to fit on straight needles, change to circular needle and work backwards and forwards in rows.)
Place markers at both ends of last row to denote base of armhole openings.
Cont straight until back meas 28 [29: 29: 30: 30] cm from markers, ending with RS facing for next row.

Shape back neck
Next row (RS): K130 [140: 150: 158: 166] and turn, leaving rem sts on a holder.
Work each side of neck separately.
Cont straight until work meas 4 [4: 5: 5: 6] cm from dividing row, ending with RS facing for next row.

Shape shoulder
Break yarn and leave sts on a holder.
With RS facing, slip centre 64 [64: 66: 66: 68] sts onto another holder, rejoin appropriate yarn to rem sts, K to end.
Complete to match first side, reversing shapings.

FRONT
Right tie and hemband
Using 2¾mm (US 2) needles and yarn A cast on 141 [148: 156: 164: 173] sts.
Work in g st for 17 rows, ending with **WS** facing for next row.
Next row (WS): K59 [66: 74: 82: 91], cast off rem 82 sts (for tie).

Break yarn and leave rem 59 [66: 74: 82: 91] sts on a holder.

Centre edging

Using 2¾mm (US 2) needles and yarn A cast on 82 sts.

Work in g st for 2 rows, ending with RS facing for next row.

Break yarn and leave sts on another holder.

Left tie and hemband

Using 2¾mm (US 2) needles and yarn A cast on 141 [148: 156: 164: 173] sts.

Work in g st for 17 rows, ending with **WS** facing for next row.

Next row (WS): Cast off rem 82 sts (for tie), K to end. 59 [66: 74: 82: 91] sts.

Join sections

Change to 3¼ mm (US 3) needles.

Next row (RS): Using yarn B, knit across 59 [66: 74: 82: 91] sts of left hemband, then 82 sts of centre edging, then 59 [66: 74: 82: 91] sts of right hemband. 200 [214: 230: 246: 264] sts.

Next row: Using B, purl.

Beg with a K row and stripe row **3**, now work in st st in stripe sequence (see above) throughout and complete as given for back from ★★.

MAKING UP

Press as described on the information page.

Join both shoulder seams as folls: holding back and front with RS facing, cast off both sets of shoulder sts tog by taking one st from front section with corresponding st from back section.

Neckband

With RS facing, using 2¾mm (US 2) circular needle and yarn A, beg and ending at left shoulder seam, pick up and knit 11 [11: 14: 14: 16] sts down left side of front neck, place marker on right needle, K across 64 [64: 66: 66: 68] sts on front holder, place marker on right needle, pick up and knit 11 [11: 14: 14: 16] sts up right side of front neck, and 11 [11: 14: 14: 16] sts down right side of back neck, place marker on right needle, K across 64 [64: 66: 66: 68] sts on back holder, place marker on right needle, then pick up and knit 11 [11: 14: 14: 16] sts up left side of back neck. 172 [172: 188: 188: 200] sts.

Round 1: ★K to within 2 sts of marker, K2tog tbl, slip marker onto right needle, K2tog, rep from ★ 3 times more, K to end.

Round 2: Purl.

Rep last 2 rounds 4 times more, then round 1 again. 124 [124: 140: 140: 152] sts.

Cast off **purlwise** (on RS).

Armhole borders (both alike)

With RS facing, using 2¾mm (US 2) needles and yarn A, pick up and knit 172 [178: 184: 190: 194] sts evenly along armhole opening row-end edges between markers.

Work in g st for 8 rows, ending with **WS** facing for next row.

Cast off knitwise (on **WS**).

See information page for finishing instructions, neatly sewing row-end edges of centre edging in place behind ties.

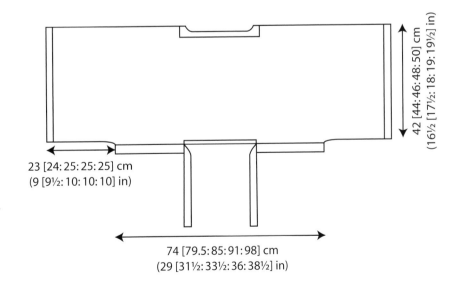

23 [24: 25: 25: 25] cm
(9 [9½: 10: 10: 10] in)

42 [44: 46: 48: 50] cm
(16½ [17½: 18: 19: 19½] in)

74 [79.5: 85: 91: 98] cm
(29 [31½: 33½: 36: 38½] in)

Main Image Page 16

Pineapple ✳✳
By Lisa Richardson

SIZE

	S	M	L	XL	XXL	
To fit bust						
	81–86	91–97	102–107	112–117	122–127	cm
	32–34	36–38	40–42	44–46	48–50	in

YARN

Rowan Panama

10	11	12	13	15	x 50gm

(photographed in Daisy 301)

NEEDLES

1 pair 2¾ mm (no 12) (US 2) needles
1 pair 3¼ mm (no 10) (US 3) needles

TENSION

27 sts and 36 rows to 10 cm measured over st st using 3¼ mm (US 3) needles.

BACK

Using 3¼ mm (US 3) needles cast on 243 [261: 281: 305: 329] sts.
Row 1 (RS): K1, ★P1, K1, rep from ★ to end.
Row 2: As row 1.
These 2 rows form moss st.
Work in moss st for a further 2 rows, ending with RS facing for next row.
Row 5 (RS): K1, P1, K to last 2 sts, P1, K1.
Row 6: K1, P1, K1, P to last 3 sts, K1, P1, K1.
Last 2 rows set the sts – edge 3 sts at both sides still in moss st with all other sts now in st st.
Cont as set until back meas 25 [26: 27: 28: 29] cm, ending with RS facing for next row.
Place markers at both ends of last row.
Cast off 69 [72: 74: 77: 80] sts at beg of next 2 rows. 105 [117: 133: 151: 169] sts.
Change to 2¾ mm (US 2) needles.
Next row (RS): K7 [7: 9: 10: 11], M1, (K2, M1) 45 [51: 57: 65: 73] times, K8 [8: 10: 11: 12]. 151 [169: 191: 217: 243] sts.
Next row: P1, ★K1, P1, rep from ★ to end.
Next row: K1, ★P1, K1, rep from ★ to end.

Last 2 rows form rib.
Cont in rib, shaping side seams by dec 1 st at each end of 2nd and 4 foll 4th rows. 141 [159: 181: 207: 233] sts.
Work 11 rows, ending with RS facing for next row.
Inc 1 st at each end of next and 2 foll 6th rows. 147 [165: 187: 213: 239] sts.
Work 5 rows, ending with RS facing for next row.
Change to 3¼ mm (US 3) needles.
Next row (RS): K8 [8: 10: 11: 12], K2tog, (K1, K2tog) 43 [49: 55: 63: 71] times, K8 [8: 10: 11: 12]. 103 [115: 131: 149: 167] sts.
Beg with a P row, now work in st st throughout as folls:★★
Inc 1 st at each end of 6th and 6 foll 6th rows. 117 [129: 145: 163: 181] sts.
Work 11 rows, ending with RS facing for next row. (Back should meas 52 [53: 54: 55: 56] cm.)
Shape armholes
Cast off 9 [10: 11: 12: 13] sts at beg of next 2 rows. 99 [109: 123: 139: 155] sts.
Dec 1 st at each end of next 9 [9: 11: 13: 15] rows, then on foll 8 [10: 11: 13: 15] alt rows. 65 [71: 79: 87: 95] sts.
Cont straight until armhole meas 18 [19: 20: 21: 22] cm, ending with RS facing for next row.
Shape shoulders and back neck
Next row (RS): Cast off 3 [5: 6: 8: 9] sts, K until there are 7 [8: 9: 11: 13] sts on right needle and turn, leaving rem sts on a holder.
Work each side of neck separately.
Cast off 3 sts at beg of next row.
Cast off rem 4 [5: 6: 8: 10] sts.
With RS facing, rejoin yarn to rem sts, cast off centre 45 [45: 49: 49: 51] sts, K to end.
Complete to match first side, reversing shapings.

FRONT

Work as given for back to ★★.
Divide for neck
Next row (WS): P68 [74: 82: 91: 100], K1, P1, K1 and slip these 71 [77: 85: 94: 103] sts onto a holder for right front (leaving yarn attached), join in new ball of yarn and cast on 39 sts, work across these sts as folls: K1, P1, K1, then P to end of row. 71 [77: 85: 94: 103] sts.
Work each side of neck separately.
Next row (RS): K to last 5 sts, K2tog (for front slope dec), K1, P1, K1.
Next row: K1, P1, K1, P to end.

These 2 rows set the sts – front slope 3 sts in moss st and all other sts in st st – and set front slope decreases.

Working all front slope decreases as set, dec 1 st at front slope of next and foll 24 alt rows **and at same time** inc 1 st at side seam edge of 3rd and 6 foll 6th rows. 52 [58: 66: 75: 84] sts.

Work 1 row, ending with RS facing for next row.

Shape armhole

Cast off 9 [10: 11: 12: 13] sts at beg and dec 1 st at end of next row. 42 [47: 54: 62: 70] sts.

Work 1 row.

Dec 1 st at armhole edge of next 9 [9: 11: 13: 15] rows, then on foll 8 [10: 11: 13: 15] alt rows **and at same time** dec 1 st at front slope edge of next and foll 2 [0: 2: 0: 0] alt rows, then on 5 [7: 7: 9: 11] foll 4th rows. 17 [20: 22: 26: 28] sts.

Dec 1 st at front slope edge **only** on 4th [4th: 4th: 2nd: 4th] and 6 [6: 6: 6: 5] foll 4th rows. 10 [13: 15: 19: 22] sts.

Cont straight until left front matches back to beg of shoulder shaping, ending with RS facing for next row.

Shape shoulder

Cast off 3 [5: 6: 8: 9] sts at beg of next row, then 4 [5: 6: 8: 10] sts at beg of foll alt row.

Cont in moss st on rem 3 sts for a further 9 [9: 10: 10: 10.5] cm (for back neck border extension), ending with RS facing for next row.

Cast off.

With RS facing, rejoin yarn to rem sts and cont as folls:

Next row (RS): K1, P1, K1, sl 1, K1, psso (for front slope dec), K to end.

Next row: P to last 3 sts, K1, P1, K1.

Complete to match left front, reversing shapings.

MAKING UP

Press as described on the information page.

Join both shoulder seams using back stitch, or mattress stitch if preferred. Join cast-off edges of back neck border extensions, then sew in place to back neck edge. Sew cast-on edge of left front in place behind right front at top of waist ribbing.

Armhole borders (both alike)

With RS facing and using 2¾ mm (US 2) needles, pick up and knit 115 [123: 129: 137: 145] sts evenly all round armhole edge.

Work in moss st as given for back for 3 rows, ending with RS facing for next row.

Cast off in moss st.

See information page for finishing instructions, leaving side seams open below markers.

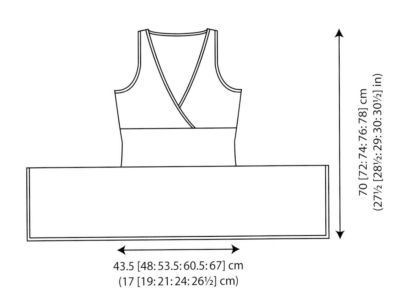

70 [72: 74: 76: 78] cm
(27½ [28½: 29: 30: 30½] in)

43.5 [48: 53.5: 60.5: 67] cm
(17 [19: 21: 24: 26½] cm)

Main Image Page 10

Prickly Pear ❋❋
By Marie Wallin

YARN

	S	M	L	XL	XXL	
To fit bust						
	81-86	91-97	102-107	112-117	122-127	cm
	32-34	36-38	40-42	44-46	48-50	in

Rowan Panama

11	12	13	14	16	x 50gm

(photographed in Cosmos 303)

NEEDLES

1 pair 2¾ mm (no 12) (US 2) needles
1 pair 3¼ mm (no 10) (US 3) needles

TENSION

23 sts and 40 rows to 10 cm measured over patt using 3¼ mm (US 3) needles.

Pattern note: The number of sts varies whilst working patt. Do NOT count sts after RS rows. All st counts given relate to original number of sts and do NOT include sts made on RS rows. When working shaping through patt, place markers 1 patt rep (4 sts) in from ends of rows. Work sts before and after markers in st st, keeping sts between markers in patt.

BACK

Using 3¼ mm (US 3) needles cast on 116 [128: 140: 156: 172] sts.
Work in g st for 2 rows, ending with RS facing for next row.
Now work in patt as folls:
Row 1 (RS): K2, ★yfwd, K4, rep from ★ to last 2 sts, yfwd, K2.
Row 2: P2tog, ★(K1, P1) into next yfwd, (P2tog) twice, rep from ★ to last 3 sts, (K1, P1) into next yfwd, P2tog.
Row 3: K4, ★yfwd, K4, rep from ★ to end.
Row 4: P2, P2tog, ★(K1, P1) into next yfwd, (P2tog) twice, rep from ★ to last 5 sts, (K1, P1) into next yfwd, P2tog, P2.
These 4 rows form patt.
Cont in patt until back meas 8 [9: 10: 11: 12] cm, ending with RS facing for next row.
Keeping patt correct, dec 1 st at each end of next and 4 foll 14th rows.
106 [118: 130: 146: 162] sts. (See pattern note.)

Work 15 rows, ending with RS facing for next row.
Inc 1 st at each end of next and 4 foll 12th rows, taking inc sts into st st until there are sufficient to work in patt. 116 [128: 140: 156: 172] sts.
Cont straight until back meas 42 [43: 44: 45: 46] cm, ending with RS facing for next row.

Shape armholes

Keeping patt correct, cast off 5 [6: 7: 8: 9] sts at beg of next 2 rows.
106 [116: 126: 140: 154] sts.
Dec 1 st at each end of next 5 [7: 7: 9: 9] rows, then on foll 4 [5: 7: 8: 11] alt rows. 88 [92: 98: 106: 114] sts.
Cont straight until armhole meas 22 [23: 24: 25: 26] cm, ending after patt row 4 and with RS facing for next row.

Shape shoulders and back neck

Cast off 6 [7: 8: 9: 10] sts at beg of next 2 rows. 76 [78: 82: 88: 94] sts.
Next row (RS): Cast off 6 [7: 8: 9: 10] sts, patt until there are 11 [11: 11: 13: 14] sts on right needle and turn, leaving rem sts on a holder.
Work each side of neck separately.
Cast off 4 sts at beg of next row.
Cast off rem 7 [7: 7: 9: 10] sts.
With RS facing, rejoin yarn to rem sts, cast off centre 42 [42: 44: 44: 46] sts, patt to end.
Complete to match first side, reversing shapings.

FRONT

Work as given for back until 14 [14: 16: 16: 18] rows less have been worked than on back to beg of shoulder shaping, ending with RS facing for next row.

Shape front neck

Next row (RS): Patt 29 [31: 34: 38: 42] sts and turn, leaving rem sts on a holder.
Work each side of neck separately.
Keeping patt correct, dec 1 st at neck edge of next 8 rows, then on foll 2 [2: 3: 3: 4] alt rows. 19 [21: 23: 27: 30] sts.
Work 1 row, ending with RS facing for next row.

Shape shoulder

Cast off 6 [7: 8: 9: 10] sts at beg of next and foll alt row.
Work 1 row.
Cast off rem 7 [7: 7: 9: 10] sts.

With RS facing, rejoin yarn to rem sts, cast off centre 30 sts, patt to end. Complete to match first side, reversing shapings.

SLEEVES

Using 3¼ mm (US 3) needles cast on 56 [56: 60: 60: 64] sts.

Work in g st for 2 rows, ending with RS facing for next row.

Now work in patt as given for back, shaping sides by inc 1 st at each end of 5th and every foll 6th row to 76 [88: 88: 104: 108] sts, then on every foll 8th row until there are 96 [100: 104: 108: 112] sts, taking inc sts into st st until there are sufficient to work in patt.

Cont straight until sleeve meas 40 [41: 42: 42: 42] cm, ending with RS facing for next row.

Shape top

Keeping patt correct, cast off 5 [6: 7: 8: 9] sts at beg of next 2 rows. 86 [88: 90: 92: 94] sts.

Dec 1 st at each end of next 7 rows, then on every foll alt row to 60 sts, then on foll 17 rows, ending with RS facing for next row. 26 sts.

Cast off 4 sts at beg of next 2 rows.

Cast off rem 18 sts.

MAKING UP

Press as described on the information page.

Join right shoulder seam using back stitch, or mattress stitch if preferred.

Neckband

With RS facing and using 2¾ mm (US 2) needles, pick up and knit 14 [14: 16: 16: 18] sts down left side of neck, 35 sts from front, 14 [14: 16: 16: 18] sts up right side of neck, then 58 [58: 60: 60: 62] sts from back. 121 [121: 127: 127: 133] sts.

Work in g st for 2 rows, ending with **WS** facing for next row.

Cast off knitwise (on **WS**).

See information page for finishing instructions, setting in sleeves using the set-in method.

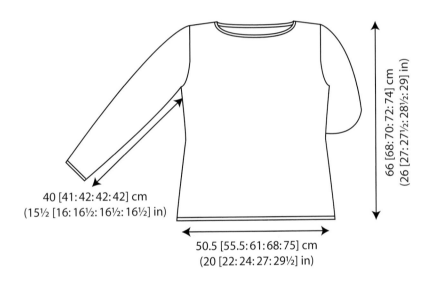

40 [41: 42: 42: 42] cm
(15½ [16: 16½: 16½: 16½] in)

50.5 [55.5: 61: 68: 75] cm
(20 [22: 24: 27: 29½] in)

66 [68: 70: 72: 74] cm
(26 [27: 27½: 28½: 29] in)

Information

TENSION

Obtaining the correct tension is perhaps the single factor which can make the difference between a successful garment and a disastrous one. It controls both the shape and size of an article, so any variation, however slight, can distort the finished garment.

Different designers feature in our books and it is **their** tension, given at the **start** of each pattern, which you must match. We recommend that you knit a square in pattern and/or stocking stitch (depending on the pattern instructions) of perhaps 5 - 10 more stitches and 5 - 10 more rows than those given in the tension note. Mark out the central 10cm square with pins. If you have too many stitches to 10cm try again using thicker needles, if you have too few stitches to 10cm try again using finer needles. Once you have achieved the correct tension your garment will be knitted to the measurements indicated in the size diagram shown at the end of the pattern.

SIZING & SIZE DIAGRAM NOTE

The instructions are given for the smallest size. Where they vary, work the figures in brackets for the larger sizes. **One set of figures refers to all sizes.** Included with most patterns in this magazine is a 'size diagram', of the finished garment and its dimensions. The measurement shown at the bottom of each 'size diagram' shows the garment width 2.5cm below the armhole shaping. To help you choose the size of garment to knit please refer to the sizing guide on page 68.

CHART NOTE

Many of the patterns in the book are worked from charts. Each square on a chart represents a stitch and each line of squares a row of knitting. Each colour used is given a different letter and these are shown in the **materials** section, or in the **key** alongside the chart of each pattern. When working from the charts, read odd rows (K) from right to left and even rows (P) from left to right, unless otherwise stated. When working lace from a chart it is important to note that all but the largest size may have to alter the first and last few stitches in order not to lose or gain stitches over the row.

WORKING A LACE PATTERN

When working a lace pattern it is important to remember that if you are unable to work both the increase and corresponding decrease and vica versa, the stitches should be worked in stocking stitch.

FINISHING INSTRUCTIONS

After working for hours knitting a garment, it seems a great pity that many garments are spoiled because such little care is taken in the pressing and finishing process. Follow the text below for a truly professional-looking garment.

PRESSING

Block out each piece of knitting and following the instructions on the ball band press the garment pieces, omitting the ribs. Tip: Take special care to press the edges, as this will make sewing up both easier and neater. If the ball band indicates that the fabric is not to be pressed, then covering the blocked out fabric with a damp white cotton cloth and leaving it to stand will have the desired effect. Darn in all ends neatly along the selvage edge or a colour join, as appropriate.

STITCHING

When stitching the pieces together, remember to match areas of colour and texture very carefully where they meet. Use a seam stitch such as back stitch or mattress stitch for all main knitting seams and join all ribs and neckband with mattress stitch, unless otherwise stated.

CONSTRUCTION

Having completed the pattern instructions, join left shoulder and neckband seams as detailed above. Sew the top of the sleeve to the body of the garment using the method detailed in the pattern, referring to the appropriate guide:

Straight cast-off sleeves: Place centre of cast-off edge of sleeve to shoulder seam. Sew top of sleeve to body, using markers as guidelines where applicable.

Square set-in sleeves: Place centre of cast-off edge of sleeve to shoulder seam. Set sleeve head into armhole, the straight sides at top of sleeve to form a neat right-angle to cast-off sts at armhole on back and front.

Shallow set-in sleeves: Place centre of cast off edge of sleeve to shoulder seam. Match decreases at beg of armhole shaping to decreases at top of sleeve. Sew sleeve head into armhole, easing in shapings.

Set-in sleeves: Place centre of cast-off edge of sleeve to shoulder seam. Set in sleeve, easing sleeve head into armhole.

Join side and sleeve seams.
Slip stitch pocket edgings and linings into place.
Sew on buttons to correspond with buttonholes.
Ribbed welts and neckbands and any areas of garter stitch should not be pressed.

Buttons in this brochure are Sourced from Bedecked.
Bedecked Limited, 1 Castle Wall, Back Fold, Hay-on-Wye, Via Hereford, HR3 5EQ

www.bedecked.co.uk
Shop tel: 01497 822769
Email: thegirls@bedecked.co.uk

Experience Ratings

✽

Easy, straight forward knitting

✽ ✽

Suitable for the average knitter

✽ ✽ ✽

For the more experienced knitter

K	knit		RS	right side
P	purl		WS	wrong side
st(s)	stitch(es)		sl 1	slip one stitch
inc	increas(e)(ing)		psso	pass slipped stitch over
dec	decreas(e)(ing)		p2sso	pass 2 slipped stitches over
st st	stocking stitch (1 row K, 1 row P)		tbl	through back of loop
g st	garter stitch (K every row)		M1	make one stitch by picking up horizontal loop before next stitch and knitting into back of it
beg	begin(ning)			
foll	following		M1P	make one stitch by picking up horizontal loop before next stitch and purling into back of it
rem	remain(ing)			
rev st st	reverse stocking stitch (1 row K , 1 row P)		yfwd	yarn forward
rep	repeat		yrn	yarn round needle
alt	alternate		meas	measures
cont	continue		0	no stitches, times or rows
patt	pattern		-	no stitches, times or rows for that size
tog	together		yo	yarn over needle
mm	millimetres		yfrn	yarn forward round needle
cm	centimetres		wyib	with yarn at back
in(s)	inch(es)		sl2togK	slip 2 stitches together knitways

CROCHET TERMS

UK crochet terms and abbreviations have been used throughout. The list below gives the US equivalent where they vary.

ABBREV.	UK	US
dc	double crochet	single crochet
htr	half treble	half double crochet
tr	treble	double crochet
dtr	double treble	treble

Sizing Guide

Our sizing now conforms to standard clothing sizes. Therefore if you buy a standard size 12 in clothing, then our size 12 or medium patterns will fit you perfectly. Dimensions in the charts shown are body measurements, not garment dimensions, therefore please refer to the measuring guide to help you to determine which is the best size for you to knit.

CASUAL SIZING GUIDE FOR WOMEN

As there are some designs that are intended to fit more generously, we have introduced our casual sizing guide. The designs that fall into this group can be recognised by the size range: Small, Medium, Large & Xlarge. Each of these sizes cover two sizes from the standard sizing guide, ie. Size S will fit sizes 8/10, size M will fit sizes 12/14 and so on. The sizing within this chart is also based on the larger size within the range, ie. M will be based on size 14.

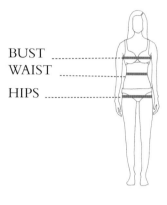

BUST ....
WAIST ....
HIPS ....

UK SIZE DUAL SIZE	S 8/10	M 12/14	L 16/18	XL 20/22	XXL 24/26	
To fit bust	32 – 34	36 – 38	40 – 42	44 – 46	48-50	inches
	81 – 86	91 - 97	102 – 107	112 – 117	122/127	cm
To fit waist	24 – 26	28 – 30	32 – 34	36 – 38	40-42	inches
	61 – 66	71 – 76	81 – 86	91 – 97	102-107	cm
To fit hips	34 – 36	38 – 40	42 – 44	46 – 48	50-52	inches
	86 – 91	97 – 102	107 – 112	117 – 122	127-132	cm

MEASURING GUIDE

For maximum comfort and to ensure the correct fit when choosing a size to knit, please follow the tips below when checking your size.

Measure yourself close to your body, over your underwear and don't pull the tape measure too tight!

Bust/chest – measure around the fullest part of the bust/chest and across the shoulder blades.

Waist – measure around the natural waistline, just above the hip bone.

Hips – measure around the fullest part of the bottom.

If you don't wish to measure yourself, note the size of a favourite jumper that you like the fit of. Our sizes are now comparable to the clothing sizes from the major high street retailers, so if your favourite jumper is a size Medium or size 12, then our casual size Medium and standard size 12 should be approximately the same fit.

To be extra sure, measure your favourite jumper and then compare these measurements with the Rowan size diagram given at the end of the individual instructions.

Finally, once you have decided which size is best for you, please ensure that you achieve the tension required for the design you wish to knit.

Remember if your tension is too loose, your garment will be bigger than the pattern size and you may use more yarn. If your tension is too tight, your garment could be smaller than the pattern size and you will have yarn left over.

Furthermore if your tension is incorrect, the handle of your fabric will be too stiff or floppy and will not fit properly. It really does make sense to check your tension before starting every project.

AUSTRALIA: Australian Country Spinners Pty Ltd, Level 7, 409 St. Kilda Road, Melbourne 3004. Tel: 03 9380 3830
Email: tkohut@auspinners.com.au

AUSTRIA: Coats Harlander GmbH, Autokaderstrasse 31, Wien A -1210.
Tel: (01) 27716

BELGIUM: Coats Benelux, Ring Oost 14A, Ninove, 9400
Tel: 054 318989 Email: sales.coatsninove@coats.com

CANADA: Westminster Fibers, 8 Shelter Drive, Greer, South Carolina, 29650
Tel: 800 445-9276 Email: info@westminsterfibers.com
Web: www.westminsterfibers.com

CHINA: Coats Shanghai Ltd, No 9 Building , Baosheng Road, Songjiang Industrial Zone, Shanghai.
Tel: 86 21 5774 3733 Email: victor.li@coats.com

DENMARK: Coats HP A/S, Tagensvej 85C, St.tv., Copenhagen
Tel: 45 35 86 90 49

FINLAND: Coats Opti Crafts Oy, Ketjutie 3, Kerava , 04220
Tel: (358) 9 274871
Email: coatsopti@coats.com Web: wwwcoatscrafts.fi

FRANCE: Coats Steiner, 100 Avenue du Général de Gaulle, Mehun-Sur-Yèvre, 18500
Tel: 02 48 23 12 30 Web: www.coatscrafts.fr

GERMANY: Coats GmbH, Kaiserstrasse 1, Kenzingen, 79341
Tel: 07162-14346 Web: www.coatsgmbh.de

HOLLAND: Coats Benelux, Ring Oost 14A, Ninove, 9400, Belgium
Tel: 0346 35 37 00 Email: sales.coatsninove@coats.com

HONG KONG: Coats Shanghai Ltd, No 8 Building , Export & Processing Garden, Songjiang Industrial Zone, Shanghai, China.
Tel: (86- 21) 57743733-326 Email: victor.li@coats.com

ICELAND: Rowan At Storkurinn, Laugavegur 59, Reykjavik, 101
Tel: 551 8258 Email: storkurinn@simnet.is Web: www.storkurinn.is

ISRAEL: Beit Hasidkit, Ms. Offra Tzenger, Sokolov St No 2, Kfar Sava, 44256
Tel: (972) 9 7482381

ITALY: Coats cucirini srl,Viale sarca no 223, Milano, 20126

KOREA: Coats Korea Co. Lt, 5F Eyeon B/D, 935-40 Bangbae-Dong, Seocho-Gu, Seoul, 137-060
Tel: 82-2-521-6262 Web: www.coatskorea.co.kr

LEBANON: y.knot, Saifi Village, Mkhalissiya Street 162, Beirut
Tel: (961) 1 992211 Email: y.knot@cyberia.net.lb

LUXEMBOURG: Coats Benelux, Ring Oost 14A, Ninove, 9400, Belgium
Tel: 0346 35 37 00 Email: sales.coatsninove@coats.com

MALTA: John Gregory Ltd, 8 Ta'Xbiex Sea Front, Msida, MSD 1512, Malta
Tel: +356 2133 0202 Email: raygreg@onvol.net

NEW ZEALAND: ACS New Zealand, 1 March Place, Belfast, Christchurch
Tel: 64-3-323-6665

NORWAY: Coats Knappehuset AS, Pb 100, Ulset, Bergen, 5873
Tel: 55 53 93 00

PORTUGAL: Coats & Clark, Quinta de Cravel, Apartado 444, Vila Nova de Gaia 4431-968 Tel: 223770700 Web: www.crafts.com.pt

SINGAPORE: Golden Dragon Store, 101 Upper Cross Street, #02-51, People's Park Centre, 058357, Singapore
Tel: (65) 65358454/65358234 Email: gdscraft@hotmail.com

SOUTH AFRICA: Arthur Bales Ltd, 62 Fourth Avenue, Linden, Johannesburg, 2195
Tel: (27) 118 882 401 Email: arthurb@new.co.za
Web: www.arthurbales.co.za

SPAIN: Coats Fabra, SA, Santa Adria, 20, Barcelona, 08030
Tel: (34) 93 290 84 00 Email: atencion.clientes@coats.com
Web: www.coatscrafts.es

SWEDEN: Coats Expotex AB, JA Wettergrensgata 7, Vastra Frolunda, Goteborg, 431 30
Tel: (46) 33 720 79 00

SWITZERLAND: Coats Stroppel AG, Turgi (AG), CH-5300
Tel: 056 298 12 20

TAIWAN: Cactus Quality Co Ltd, 7FL-2, No. 140, Sec. 2 Roosevelt Road, Taipei,Taiwan, R.O.C. 10084
Tel: 00886-2-23656527 Email:cqcl@ms17.hinet.net
Web: www.excelcraft.com.tw

THAILAND: Global Wide Trading, 10 Lad Prao Soi 88, Bangkok 10310
Tel: 00 662 933 9019
Email:TheNeedleWorld@yahoo.com – global.wide@yahoo.com

U.S.A.: Westminster Fibers Inc, 8 Shelter Drive, Greer, 29650, South Carolina
Tel: (800) 445-9276 Email: info@westminsterfibers.com
Web: www.westminsterfibers.com

U.K: Rowan, Green Lane Mill, Holmfirth,West Yorkshire, England HD9 2DX
Tel: +44 (0) 1484 681881 Email: mail@knitrowan.com
Web: www.knitrowan.com

For stockists in all other countries please contact Rowan for details

Gallery

Apricot
Pattern Page 34

Banana Wrap
Pattern Page 37

Breadfruit
Pattern Page 38

Candlenut
Pattern Page 41

Carob
Pattern Page 42

Durian
Pattern Page 46

Guava
Pattern Page 48

Kaffir Dress
Pattern Page 49

Mango
Pattern Page 52

Mangosteen
Pattern Page 54

Papaya
Pattern Page 55

Passion
Pattern Page 57

Peach
Pattern Page 60

Pineapple
Pattern Page 62

Prickly Pear
Pattern Page 64